D1005842

# FEARLESS INNOVATION

Alex Goryachev

# FEARLESS INNOVATION

## GOING BEYOND THE BUZZWORD TO CONTINUOUSLY DRIVE GROWTH, IMPROVE THE BOTTOM LINE, AND ENACT CHANGE

WILEY

Published by John Wiley & Sons, Inc., Hoboken, New Jersey.

Published simultaneously in Canada.



For general information on our other products and services or for technical support, please contact our Customer Care Department within the United States at (800) 762–2974, outside the United States at (317) 572–3993 or fax (317) 572–4002.

Wiley publishes in a variety of print and electronic formats and by print-on-demand. Some material included with standard print versions of this book may not be included in e-books or in print-on-demand. If this book refers to media such as a CD or DVD that is not included in the version you purchased, you may download this material at http://booksupport.wiley.com. For more information about Wiley products, visit www.wiley.com.

Library of Congress Cataloging-in-Publication Data

Names: Goryachev, Alex, 1975- author.
Title: Fearless innovation : going beyond the buzzword to continuously drive growth, improve the bottom line, and enact change / Alex Goryachev.
Description: Hoboken, New Jersey : Wiley, 2020. | Includes index.
Identifiers: LCCN 2019036622 (print) | LCCN 2019036623 (ebook) | ISBN 9781119579526 (hardback) | ISBN 9781119579618 (adobe pdf) | ISBN 9781119579588 (epub)
Subjects: LCSH: Disruptive technologies. | Success in business.
Classification:LCCHD45.G592020(print)|LCCHD45(ebook)|DDC 658.4/063–dc23
LC record available at https://lccn.loc.gov/2019036622
LC ebook record available at https://lccn.loc.gov/2019036623

Cover design: Wiley

Printed in the United States of America

F10016196_121119

*To my son Matthew.*
*I hope you'll always be as fearless and innovative as you are today.*
*I love you with all my heart.*

# Contents

*Acknowledgments* *ix*

*Introduction: From Buzzword to Reality* *xi*

Chapter 1 **Innovation Is Now or Never** 1

Don't Join the Dying Breeds 3

Work with Change, Not Against It 8

Know When to Take Action 14

Summary: Innovation Waits for No One 18

Chapter 2 **No Leadership = No Strategy = No Innovation** 25

Recognize How Dysfunction and Stagnation Begin 27

Take Responsibility 30

Ask Questions 32

Clarify and Publish Employee Sentiments, Goals, and Strategy 38

Summary: Lead, Strategize, Innovate 41

Chapter 3 **If You Can't Measure It, You Can't Manage It** 45

Get Real About Innovation 47

Find the Metrics 50

Incentivize Innovation through Radical Transparency 54

Time It Right 58

Summary: Metrics Matter 62

Chapter 4 **Innovation Is *Not* Disruption** 69
Stop Thinking "Disruptively" 71
Start Thinking Pragmatically 77
Get Back to the Basics 78
Summary: The Pen Is Mightier than the Program 83

Chapter 5 **The Lonely Innovator Myth** 89
Treat Innovation Like a Team Sport 92
Foster Diversity and Inclusion 97
Summary: Innovation Is a Team Sport 106

Chapter 6 **Innovation Wants to Be Free** 111
Come Together 114
Take Co-Innovation to the Next Level 119
Summary: The Freedom of the Ecosystem 128

Chapter 7 **Outcomes Must Be Orchestrated** 135
Don't Let Innovation Get Lost 137
Hire a Chief Innovation Officer 139
Put Governance Processes into Action 142
Build Innovation Teams 144
Summary: Orchestrating Invisible Innovation 149

Chapter 8 **Communicate, Communicate, Communicate** 153
Invest in Communications Skills and Capabilities 156
Start Internally 160
Create Dialogue Externally 166
Summary: Discover, Listen, Act 171

*Conclusion: Business as Usual* 177

*About the Author* 181

*Index* 183

# Acknowledgments

Many people helped make *Fearless Innovation* a reality. I could never have made it on my own this far without the support of my mentors and "co-conspirators" who pushed me to accomplish more than I have ever imagined.

Throughout my career, I've worked for truly unique leaders, such as Gerald T. Halpin, Chris Thompson, Paul Stark, Ronald Acra, Hina Patel, Brent Wahl, Venkat Narayanan, David Ward, and Gene Hall. I want to thank all of them for supporting my aspirations, and helping me discover and develop my true potential. I owe a special debt of gratitude to Maciej Kranz for encouraging me to pursue what's possible, including writing this book.

When it comes to changing culture, most of my work would be impossible without the courage, leadership, and perseverance of Mathilde Durvy, who partnered with me to take employee innovation programs to new levels and to then establish them as the best in the industry. I am also fortunate to be surrounded by fearless trailblazers who always inspire me to change the status quo. I am indebted to Jenn Loftin, who always proved that innovation can indeed blossom when supported by the right structure, discipline, and governance. My special gratitude goes to Anna Gnatyuk and Jenny Agustin for believing in me and joining me on this innovation adventure. I am lucky to have amazing friends and co-workers who have supported me through my journey-thank you Olga Beregovaya, Lindy Bartell, Miroslav Sarbaev, John Parello, Michael Maltese, Wayne Cuervo, Andrey Kozlov, Gulia Trombini, Marc Musgrove, Simon Gladin, Masha Finkelstein, Dave Maslana, Chris Melching, Mikhail Pakhomov, Roman Kostin, Alex Hills, Irina Kosinovsky, Zhenya Kurts, Flora

Freitas, Tatyana Rudchenko, Yuri Naumov, Guillaume De Saint Marc, Marina Velednitsky, Tom Kneen, Elena Ropaeva, Nick Chrissos, Yelena Denisova, Peter Shearman, Vadim Stepanchenko, Boris Fomitchev, Oseas Ramirez Assad and Cayla Young.

Wendy Khentigan and Marla Flores Reves deserve special recognition for helping me focus on what's important in my life, which made writing this book much more joyful and rewarding.

Finally, none of this would have possible without the help of my family, most importantly my wife, Maria, and my son, Matthew. Words cannot express how much I appreciate Maria's and Matthew's encouragement, understanding, support, and pure unconditional love. I am also grateful to my parents, Yuri and Tamara, and my sister, Julia, who has always inspired me to seek change and adventure over safety and comfort.

The task of turning this book into reality is shared by so many people, which includes tremendous support from Mark Nelson, Mat Miller, and Zachary Schisgal, Vicki Adang, Amy Handy, Jocelyn Kwiatkowski, and Jenny Douglas. Scott Kirsner, cofounder and editor of *Innovation Leader* magazine, graciously provided invaluable guidance and archival resources that were essential in researching this book.

And last, but not least, I am grateful to Zach Gajewski, the most amazing editor in the world, who spent countless hours with me bringing this book to life.

# Introduction: From Buzzword to Reality

Innovation is a horrible word.

The term has become so buzzy, it seems to have lost all practical meaning. Ask a hundred people to define it and you'll receive just as many different answers. And, you know what? All of these answers might be right—or they might be wrong.

This is, in part, due to the fact that discussions about the topic are everywhere today. If you actually google "What is innovation?" you will receive nearly half a million results, and according to Google Trends, the number of search requests for news related to "innovation" tripled between 2014 and 2019.[1] Not a day goes by without another dozen articles, blog posts, or think pieces on the concept, highlighting how we all need to be more innovative and showcasing the latest process and methodology that should be immediately adopted. We read, listen, and try to keep up, looking for clarity and some type of real-world application of what is seen as a squishy subject with no end.

Today, 63 percent of companies are hiring chief innovation officers, and more than 90 percent of companies are implementing new tech to support innovation processes.[2] Sure, that's great, but there's a problem here: despite the obvious growth of demand for "innovation," we remain utterly confused about the concept. In the meantime, most leaders believe that dropping the word into a shareholder letter from time to time or mentioning it at a quarterly employee all-hands meeting is enough to prove that they're on top of the trend. Let me let you in on a little secret: they're not.

Many of these organizations relegate innovation to one very special team somewhere in the "hip" part of the office, featuring free snacks and "edgy" motivational posters, and they think they've done their job—innovation is enabled; time to celebrate! It's understandable. With so much information out there on the topic, it's hard to know where to start, let alone with what goal and for what purpose, even for the "practitioners" themselves. Leaders are enthusiastic about encouraging everyone to be innovative, yet vague about what this means in practical terms. In return, employees have little interest in something that their bosses don't know what to do with or can't even describe.

But why does this matter? If "innovation" is such a buzzword, what's the point? And why in the hell are you reading another book on the topic? Why not stick to business as usual and just ask marketing and PR to make your company appear more innovative? Innovation is an amorphous concept anyhow, the business jargon du jour, the latest flavor of the month. In short, a bunch of bullshit. Right?

Well, I'm here to tell you that though innovation can be confusing, misunderstood, and even pull-your-hair-out frustrating at times (just take a look at my author photo), it is, in fact, far from bullshit. Throughout the centuries, it has been at the core of human aspirations and essential to the world's most successful companies, organizations, cities, and countries. Innovation is the only proven path to business growth and societal impact, whether measured in money or happiness. It's not a "nice-to-have"—it's a necessity.

If leaders refuse innovation, then it disappears in the cracks, left without clear purpose, unmeasured and unaccountable. Even if they give it lip service, without action and reinforcement, it goes nowhere and actually sets organizations on a dangerous and eventually self-destructive path. But when leaders embrace innovation and welcome change, well, that's another story.

## Living with Change

I'm no stranger when it comes to dealing with change. After all, I was born in a place that no longer exists—the USSR. When I was sixteen years old, I witnessed my home country, one of the most powerful in the world at the time, collapse practically overnight, affecting nearly 300 million people and generating sudden economic and societal shifts that will continue to have an impact for generations to come.

Later in my teens, I was transplanted to the United States. Suddenly, I was exposed to shockingly different societal and economic norms than those I had been used to, and I felt a little lost, uncertain where I fit in. I longed for some type of purpose, meaningful connection, and freedom of self-expression that I couldn't find at first. My English and overall social skills weren't the greatest, so I invested my time in teaching myself the Linux operating system, hung out with a local hacking community of fellow weird outcasts, and became a supporter of the Electronic Frontier Foundation, a groundbreaking nonprofit that was the first to understand the importance of civil liberties and personal privacy in cyberspace. These were the best choices I've ever made.

During the early dot-com days, I was lucky to experience the community spirit of Silicon Valley before the boom. I was warmly welcomed in California by a diverse group of free-thinking technology professionals from around the world, and I invested my days and nights in projects that came to define and shape the future of digital entertainment and the music industry.

In addition to co-founding and launching a music touring and production company, I found my tribe and worked nonstop at Liquid Audio, a startup that pioneered a new business model for the music industry, allowing consumers to purchase high-quality music content online, while ensuring artists and labels still got paid. Later, I went to the "dark side" and practically moved in to Napster's offices, the largest and most controversial online music service of the early 2000s. They were being sued by Metallica, one of my favorite bands at the time, as well as the Record Industry Association of America (RIAA), which was worth billions of dollars, and I was there to help Napster change their technology architecture and business model while they raced against the clock to survive.

Fast forward a decade, and I landed at Cisco, leading the company's Co-Innovation Centers, setting strategy, and, more importantly, driving co-innovation with startups, key customers, and channel partners, as well as with cities and governments in fourteen countries. These award-winning innovation programs also provide employees, at all levels, with the opportunity to share and implement their biggest and brightest ideas. Even better, they ensure that the rest of the company actively supports these employees in these endeavors.

Besides leading the overall co-innovation strategy at Cisco in the Corporate Development and Strategy team, I've worked in numerous areas of the company, contributing to its success and helping to shape its approach to innovation throughout the enterprise. Starting in sales, I worked on ecosystem enablement, then moved to global marketing in an effort to streamline global operations. Among other departments, I also held positions in corporate finance, working on business transformation, and in engineering, developing new emerging technologies and business models. These experiences have provided me with a 360-degree view of how the World's #1 Workplace operates, innovates, and succeeds.[3]

Having given hundreds of presentations on innovation and spoken with thousands of people about the topic, I've had the chance to regularly share my experiences and learn from my peers around the world. Those with less hands-on experience with the topic, however, tend to ask me the same questions over and over again: Is innovation real, or is it a load of BS? If it is real, how should we innovate? How do we overcome our fear of missing out on trends or failing? Where should we focus our attention? And wait, what's innovation again?

When I answer these questions, I feel like I'm a part of a support group, and I am often the "innovation therapist." Because really, that's what most people I've spoken with need (no, not therapy, though some of us certainly do need that), but a clear, pragmatic guide—relaxed, jargon-free, and unpretentious—that will help them get over their confusion and start innovating with a sense of purpose.

## Okay, But WTF *Is* Innovation?

I'm glad you asked.

Innovation isn't a *thing*, it's a mindset and attitude made of up clear principles—those discussed throughout this book—that help individuals, organizations, and societies adapt to change, survive and grow, progress and prosper. As the world continues to evolve, innovation enables our communities, businesses, and selves to evolve with it. Innovation is more art than science, but its principles can easily be put into practice.

When truly baked into a company's culture, innovation is a constant, whether the company is working on large initiatives or small projects. Yet, keeping it alive requires focused effort—innovation is not a one-time event. It drives the survival of the fittest and, whether it is Darwinian evolution or God's plan, it is a continuous process. The only way for a company's business strategy to evolve, then, is by embracing innovation.

Change happens naturally; innovation doesn't. It can't be "checked in on" from time to time; it has to be central to any organization and understood by employees from top to bottom—nothing short of a culture of constant, conscious awareness and transformation. Otherwise, innovation will not be prioritized, meaning organizations, and their leaders, will be stuck in the present, which will quickly become the past.

Speaking of the past, innovation's nothing new either: it has been taking place since the first humans began walking upright on two feet. What's changed over millions of years, though—and what is always changing—is the environment we're innovating in, and how the concept is applied. There are now more tools than ever for innovation, but there is also more pressure from consumers, citizens, shareholders, employees, leaders, and business owners to "innovate" by any means possible. Progression is the way of the world, and organizations exist only when they serve human ambitions, meeting the demands of progress.

We've entered the Fourth Industrial Revolution, a time in which we're experiencing rapid technological, social, and cultural change. Such revolutions always shift the balance of power and create winners and losers—those businesses that can't keep up will languish and perish. For example, in 2018 the innovation consulting firm Innosight found that between 1964 and 2016, the average tenure of companies on the S&P 500 narrowed from thirty-three years to twenty-four years.[4] This tenure is forecasted to continue to shrink, down to twelve years by 2027, by which time more than three-quarters of the S&P 500 will consist of new companies that we have not yet heard of.[5]

Still, most companies don't seem that concerned. As the author and social commentator Scott Adams, of *Dilbert* fame, pointed out, "Large corporations welcome innovation and individualism in the same way the dinosaurs welcomed large meteors."[6] We can toss the word around as much as we want, but unless the concept is given the attention it deserves, we, too, will end up extinct. Most leaders, particularly middle managers, feel that they have enough to worry about as it is and tend to focus on what's in front of them at the moment. Keep the shareholders happy and the business profitable, and whoever's next in line can worry about the future. They look at innovation as something that isn't essential to their business or job, failing to realize that innovation is actually essential to *everyone's* job. Sadly, they're missing out on the new reality that foresight for the long-term is just as important as insight into the short-term.

Instead of producing a real impact, talk of innovation generates way more slogans than clear, actionable results. It also causes many leaders to enter anxiety mode. They deny the need to evolve, or they grasp at straws for a concept of innovation that either doesn't exist or is completely irrelevant for their organizations. In response, like so many of us, they turn a blind eye to what's right there in front of them, ignoring the current pace of change we're experiencing and placing their attention elsewhere. We do this in our personal and professional lives all the time, getting trapped in tactical issues, tangible problems we must address immediately, without understanding the underlying purpose, the bigger picture, or even our full potential.

## Fearless Innovation

It's time to take a breath, step back, and truly begin to understand what innovation is and what it isn't; how it can make a difference between surviving and thriving; and how it can be applied to more than just our day-to-day jobs, but also to the transformation of our businesses, our personal and professional success, and the improved conditions of our society and planet.

The principles outlined in this book aim to do just that. They're straightforward, timely, and actionable, no matter the size of your company or organization. Whether executing innovation through leadership and strategy; measuring innovation efforts or outcomes; building cross-functional, diverse teams; working with the entire ecosystem to capture bigger opportunities; or communicating the value of innovation to employees, partners, and beyond, such principles offer a blueprint to driving growth, creating clear measurable value, and enacting change. I have little interest in brainwashing you with innovation as a theoretical concept and prefer to explore the practical whys and hows. Throughout my life I've learned to question conventional wisdom, challenge authority, quickly adapt to my surroundings, and shape my own future. One might say that in the process, I've developed a highly functioning BS meter, which comes in quite handy when innovation is concerned. So all of the advice in this book is backed by experience, and when skepticism is necessary, you'll see plenty of it.

This material is not scripted in line with the "innovation management" gospel or theoretical "methodologies," those marketing phrases and complicated flowcharts that sound and look good but provide little practical substance. In many ways, I consider this guide an "antimethodology" methodology, an open process to get to the heart of innovation and show the immense impact it can have in any setting; so you won't find any flowcharts here. What we need is to see through the BS, acknowledge the reality of unending disruption, and present innovation for what it really is.

Since my early days, I've learned that change happens no matter what. We have an option of embracing it through innovation or resisting it through our own denial. It's our choice, but without open minds and focus, our attempts to create some type of meaningful impact on the world—whether in our city, communities, families, or where we work—will fall short. The only way to create a truly positive, lasting effect is by embracing change, and using it to our advantage. We all know that any lasting transformation within an organization doesn't happen quickly, as it requires a leap of faith in addition to discipline, commitment, and creativity. It won't always be easy, but that's not the point: innovation is a journey, and there is simply no future without it.

## Notes


1. Google Trends, Search Term: Innovation, https://trends.google.com/trends/explore?date=today%205-y&gprop=news&q=innovation.
2. Forbes Coaches Council, "What Can Your Organization Do to Become More Innovative?" *Forbes*, July 13, 2017, https://www.forbes.com/sites/forbescoachescouncil/2017/07/13/what-can-your-organization-do-to-become-more-innovative.
3. Rola Dagher, "#1 Best Place to Work," *Cisco Canada Blog*, October 4, 2019, https://gblogs.cisco.com/ca/2019/10/04/1-best-place-to-work/
4. Scott D. Anthony, S. Patrick Viguerie, Evan I. Schwartz, and John Van Landeghem, "2018 Corporate Longevity Forecast: Creative Destruction is Accelerating," *Innosight Executive Briefing*, February 2018, https://www.innosight.com/wp-content/uploads/2017/11/Innosight-Corporate-Longevity-2018.pdf
5. Ibid.
6. B.R., "An A–Z of Business Quotations: Innovation," *Economist*, August 17, 2012, https://www.economist.com/schumpeter/2012/08/17/innovation.

# Chapter 1

## Innovation Is Now or Never

Let's talk unicorns. No, not the mythical horse-like creature with one horn that was used as a symbol for Jesus Christ in medieval times, and depending on who you ask, poops rainbows (thanks, Squatty Potty). The unicorns I'm referring to are those privately owned startups valued at a billion dollars or more that are currently taking over the world. As recently as 2015 there were only eighty-two such companies; as of 2018 there were more than 295.[1] Fast forward just a year, and by April of 2019 there were 326, with a collective worth of almost $1.1 trillion.[2] Many of those were household names, such as 23andMe, Stripe, and SpaceX, along with Uber and Pinterest, which have since gone public. Others you may never have heard of, like the real estate broker Lianjia, the Bitcoin mining application company Bitmain Technologies, or the ByteDance Internet and AI technology company, all three of which happen to be Chinese firms.[3]

Unicorns are here because of the Fourth Industrial Revolution, which is transforming the way we live, work, and learn, unlike any changes seen before. As a modern society, we've come a long way since Britain's technological advancements in the mid-eighteenth century that led to the First Industrial Revolution, a time that may seem very quaint in comparison to today. Within a hundred years, the world would experience the start of the Second Industrial Revolution, the birth of the assembly line and mass production, not to mention the widespread use of electricity. The Third Industrial Revolution, which seems like just yesterday to many, was another leap forward, with digital manufacturing, automated production, and global Internet connectivity. Organizations had to keep up with technological progress to stay relevant. Those who particularly understood the changes around them were able to shape the world that we live in today.

We have now entered the Fourth Industrial Revolution and are experiencing change at an unprecedented pace, level, and intensity. From augmented reality to genomics, our society is becoming infused with new technologies embedded not just within our homes and workplaces, but even our bodies. We are rapidly blurring the physical and the digital, transforming the way we live and, in some sense, what it even means to be human. This transformation is just in its infancy, as business models will continue to be disrupted and access to technology will increase, along with the ability to develop, launch, and scale new products and services in an ever-shorter time span.

From the cotton spun by the British in the 1760s to the digitization of the twenty-first century, continuous innovation has been necessary for the unicorns of their day to emerge, spearhead change, and prosper. As human societies move forward, so do their businesses. Change always creates opportunities. There's no telling exactly where this hyper speed of exponential change will lead us, but if we don't act now, we'll miss out on the greatest opportunities of our lifetime.

Innovation is urgent, time sensitive, and always present. It's how we've adapted to change and succeeded over the past two and a half centuries, and long before. As with every era behind us, there are new business, social, and economic issues that must be tackled in the Fourth Industrial Revolution, and just as the challenges and opportunities of the past had to be met, so do those of today. If you want your organization to survive, remain competitive, and prosper, then you can't wait to start taking action. Otherwise, you'll be forgotten, passed up by the next in line, or blindsided by disruption, because today's unicorns could be gone tomorrow. In short, innovation never sleeps, and we can't sleep on it.

Still, despite the obvious need, many organizations lack a clear focus when it comes to innovation or fail to align their efforts with market realities. They "kind of" know that they "must innovate," yet they are not sure "where" and "why." Sadly, leadership is missing the big picture as well; most executives don't even know where their innovation priorities should lie, and by some accounts only 14 percent of executives feel "highly confident" that their organizations are prepared for the changes taking place in the Fourth Industrial Revolution.[4] Many of us simply don't know what to do.

So where do we begin?

## Don't Join the Dying Breeds

You're probably thinking that, as a rule, "don't join the dying breeds" is pretty much self-evident. Who would want to be a casualty of the Fourth Industrial Revolution, and wouldn't most leaders do all they could to avoid such a fate? It's a good point, but the truth is it doesn't always play out that way in reality, no matter our best intentions. Let me give you a simple example: We all know that exercise is key to living longer—no one would deny that. Yet the US weight-loss industry is currently valued at $72 billion and growing.[5] If we actually followed the advice of our doctors and exercised diligently, we wouldn't be spending so much on meal replacement programs, pills, and the latest, greatest diets. The US is one of the most educated nations on earth,[6] but this hasn't protected it from an obesity epidemic.[7] Despite knowledge about the benefits of exercise, and an overall desire to live longer, nearly 40 percent of Americans are obese.[8] Even though we know better, we can't seem to help ourselves; many companies that have receded into oblivion are no different. Maybe they made the effort, maybe they didn't, but one thing is for sure—they have gone extinct, some along with their entire industries, even when they, too, "knew better."

The ever-growing list of recent former industry pioneers that have quickly disappeared in this new era is well-known and well-trodden: AOL, BlackBerry, Kodak, Myspace, Motorola, Nokia, Polaroid, Sears, Toys "R" Us, Xerox, Blockbuster—it continues on and on. You can still visit the last remaining Blockbuster in the world, in Bend, Oregon, which has become a popular tourist attraction, but that's it for what was once the world's largest video rental chain.[9] This fate could have been avoided had the company's focus been on innovation, allowing leaders to see what was happening right in front of them and what was to come. In 2008, Jim Keyes, the CEO of Blockbuster at the time, told the *Motley Fool*, "Neither RedBox nor Netflix are even on the radar screen in terms of competition."[10] Of course, Keyes is not alone.

Many years ago, a recruiter asked me to consider interviewing for a small Palo Alto startup called Facebook. I laughed it off. The concept of social media already existed, and Myspace—a popular social media network at the time that once surpassed Google as the most visited website in the United States—seemed to be doing incredibly well and meeting all its customers' needs. Friggin' Myspace! When the platform ended up losing most, if not all, of the music that its users uploaded in the twelve years between 2003 and 2015 (which amounted to 53 million songs from 14.2 million artists), it was almost like nothing happened.[11] That was because by 2015, Myspace had fallen so far into obscurity, no one seemed to notice the loss of so much un-backed-up data—this was the company that I thought would make startups like Facebook completely hopeless.

Shortsightedness stifles our ability to stay relevant and contributes to a mindset that lulls us into believing that as long as everything is generally fine now, it'll be fine in the near, or distant, future as well. When it comes to the business environment, today almost always gets in front of tomorrow. Part of human nature is that as we grow older, we may be wiser (though maybe not always), but we also become self-centered and pay less attention to the changes happening around us. The same idea applies to most leaders: even when change is on the horizon, they resist it or brush it off, as if they will find shelter in this "proven" strategy that has failed so many companies before. We often don't take the time to ask "Is change coming?" let alone to answer this question. Instead, when a major shift takes place, we tend to respond in one of three ways.

### The Three (Worst) Responses to Change

The first response is to ignore it, the good ol' "stick your head in the sand and hope for the best." Perhaps no better example illustrates this tactic than the lack of timely response from brick-and-mortar retailers to online commerce. As online sales took off, the days of "hanging out" at the mall, casually shopping from store to store with a quick bite at the food court, started to fade quite quickly. Mall and department store shopping, once seen as quintessentially American pastimes, became two of the earliest casualties of the Fourth Industrial Revolution. Some stores that still inhabit these cavernous pieces of antiquity have diversified with online sales, but many retailers don't have a long-term transformation plan outside of this move, which may already be too little, too late. The retail apocalypse is only beginning: a 2019 report from the investment bank UBS found that with each 1 percent increase in online retail, up to 8,500 physical stores will need to close, leading to 75,000 stores being shuttered by 2026.[12] Sadly, instead of investing in new business models and capabilities, many retailers are just praying they aren't one of those 75,000.

The second response to change is another classic: shame it. Instead of actually doing something when change is afoot, many of us invest our efforts in resisting it by saying "it's only temporary," "it will never work," or that any unproven initiative, idea, or endeavor will be as dead as a doornail in no time. We poke fun or call its validity into question. We even ridicule it or try to laugh it off. In fact, if it's innovative, expect people to put it down.

For generations, groundbreaking innovations in music that challenge the norms have been targets of this negative, shortsighted response. Take jazz, for example. Known as "devil's music" when it first started to gain popularity and notoriety in the 1920s, its critics included Henry Ford, the *New York Times*, and Thomas Edison, who said the music sounded better when played backward.[13] As the '20s came to a close, sixty communities throughout the US had laws in place barring jazz from being played at public dances.[14] Of course, jazz's popularity only increased over time and it is now respected as one of America's most cherished art forms.

Still, a hundred years after Edison scorned the genre, even its fans and performers put down innovations within the scene itself. Take the music industry's response to one of my favorite performers, Kenny G, the innovative multiplatinum-selling musician who has been ridiculed mercilessly for his curly locks, commercialism, and "soft jazz" stylings. Kenny G is regularly looked down upon by purist jazz aficionados and acolytes alike, which is particularly funny, as "pure" jazz has stayed somewhat stagnant in recent decades. Do you think any of those detractors bother him at all? Of course not—Kenny G has sold over 75 million records.[15]

When he first found commercial success in the 1980s, Kenny G was interviewed by the *LA Times*, and he explained that even back then, he wasn't trying to relive the jazz of the past. "It's been done," he explained. "I'm into new ideas and experimentation, so it doesn't bother me if the purists don't like my music."[16] These new ideas and experimentation have led him to become the highest-selling instrumental musician in modern times. He's happy to be considered "commercial" and likes creating music similar to some of his favorite sax players of all time, including David Sanborn and Grover Washington Jr. Of the musicians, Kenny G said, "I like them because they're always innovative. You can't criticize people for having different and new ideas."[17] Disparage him as much as you want, and jazz dogmatists be damned, but innovation is at the center of Kenny G's approach to writing and playing music, and he is great at it.

The third common (and also incorrect) response to change is to try to protect the status quo through regulation, something I've experienced firsthand. While working for Napster, I witnessed the company become so disruptive that it threatened the entire recording industry—an industry, by the way, that refused to believe in the concept of digital music when it first came onto the scene (see the first response, "ignore it"). Once the Record Industry Association of America (RIAA) noticed the impact, it took legal action. In its attempts to fight the inevitable digital disruption onslaught, the RIAA did not stop at Napster; it also went after the consumers themselves, suing them for illegal downloading and file sharing. Yet these attempts proved feeble in stemming consumers from welcoming and adopting digital music. Yes, Napster never survived the litigation, but ironically, the music industry did not survive Napster either and had to adapt—the digital music revolution was unstoppable, no matter the amount of regulation.[18]

All three of these responses—ignoring, shaming, and regulating—are dangerous to the future of any organization, because they distract us from understanding and embracing change. To stay relevant, we must meet challenges, trends, and new realities head on, no matter how uncomfortable they might make us or how skeptical of or shocked by them we are. Who would have guessed, for example, that "online sports" (what is that anyway?) would be competing with traditional sports for people's attention? According to *SB Nation*, the sports blogging network owned by Vox Media (another unicorn company), in 2018, during the Overwatch League's opening weekend, their games had an average of 280,000 viewers per minute, beating out the NFL's *Thursday Night Football*'s average viewers on streaming services.[19]

*SB Nation* further reported, "At its peak, the Overwatch League had 437,000 concurrent viewers, averaging 408,000 on its opening day, according to Overwatch creators Blizzard Entertainment. In comparison the NFL had an average of 372,000 viewers on Amazon in 2017 and 243,000 on Twitter."[20] Research from 2019 actually found that come 2021, US esports will beat out every other professional sports league, aside from the NFL, in regard to viewership.[21] (A number of companies are wisely catching on, and have begun marketing in the area, including Cox Communications, Coca-Cola, and KitKat.[22])

And did you know that the highest-earning channel on YouTube in 2018 was essentially run by a seven-year-old child? (Talk about shock and surprise!) With clever orchestration from his parents, Ryan, of Ryan ToysReview, makes millions of dollars reviewing toys in online videos. That year he jumped from number 8 to number 1 on *Forbes*'s list of the highest-paid YouTube stars, earning $22 million, thanks to his 17 million followers.[23] When Steve Chen, co-founder of YouTube, sold the company to Google in 2005, he didn't see a long-term strategy for the video streaming service, stating, "There's just not that many videos I want to watch."[24] He could have never predicted Ryan, or 1.8 billion monthly users.[25]

Sports and toys—surely these aren't the great examples that embody the Fourth Industrial Revolution, right? Not so fast. Within these two areas alone, we're talking significant technological innovation, new business models, and a relentless desire to do things differently, not to mention rapid growth. Note that even though the NFL was founded in 1920 and the Overwatch League was founded almost one hundred years later in 2016, within a few years the two were already competing over viewers. Change happens in all sorts of unlikely places, whether or not we want it to or expect it to. We must avoid tunnel vision and pay attention to more than just our immediate surroundings, so we can understand and determine how to adjust to change in the most thoughtful and pragmatic manner. To do so, however, we must first get to know the factors driving change today and the new opportunities and challenges in front of us.

## Work with Change, Not Against It

The rate of acceleration in the Fourth Industrial Revolution cannot be stressed enough. Customer expectations are rapidly changing; businesses and organizations are suddenly evolving; new products and services are conquering industries practically overnight; and real-time hyper-collaboration across time zones, countries, and industries has become the norm. If we don't accept and understand these influences, we'll never be able to work with them, so it's important to identify the key drivers that are enabling the world around us. These are, of course, subject to change at nearly any time, but there are a few mainstays that have proven their longevity and look to be integral going forward into the future as well.

First, the world is becoming truly digital. According to Cisco's Visual Networking Index, by 2022 there will be so many connected devices in the world that they'll number more than three times the global population. With 3.6 networked devices per capita, this adds up to an astonishing 28.5 billion networked devices, up from 18 billion only five years prior in 2017.[26] Of course, all of these connected devices are contributing to the increase in global Internet traffic. Starting at only 100 gigabytes *per day* in 1992, in 2017 this traffic was up to 46,600 gigabytes *per second* and is expected to reach 150,700 gigabytes per second by 2022.[27] In simple terms, here's what happens in one minute on the Internet: 1 million people log in to Facebook, 4.5 million YouTube videos are viewed, 87,500 tweets are sent, 1.4 million pictures are swiped on Tinder, 3.8 million Google searches occur, and nearly $1 billion is spent on products and services.[28]

When looking at customer value, market valuation, and revenue growth rates, digital platforms are the most successful business models of our time, which include 70 percent of the top ten most valuable companies worldwide.[29] As the world is becoming more connected, it's been found that fewer than 10 percent of companies' business models will be economically viable in such a climate—and private surveys show that CEOs *know* this.[30]

The second key driver of change is that technology is becoming radically more affordable, delivering greater capabilities while requiring less space. Take data storage, for example. As a student, I remember saving for months to buy a hard drive. Today, storage is nearly free, dropping from an estimated $500,000 per gigabyte to three cents per gigabyte, from around

1982 to 2017.[31] There is a famous picture of an IBM 350 hard drive being loaded onto an airplane in 1956—the 5-megabyte hard drive weighed more than 2,000 pounds and was available at a rental price of a mere $3,200 per month. To put that in context, Apple's most popular iPhone products 6 and 6 Plus, which sold over 130 million units, were priced at $200, weighed less than one-third of a pound, and had over 3,000 times the capacity of the IBM 350.

Thanks to technology, another major influence on how we live and work today comes from a changing economic landscape. There are significantly lower barriers to entering into almost any business than there were just a few decades ago. In today's society, entrepreneurs can start their business and launch products or services seemingly instantaneously. Many no longer have to rent office space, buy assets, or even hire people, yet they can take their products global in no time.

These influences, coupled with an unprecedented access to capital, have given rise to all sorts of new businesses and ventures; from personal genomics and artificial intelligence to mobile food delivery and on-demand entertainment, we are provided with more opportunities to change our life experiences every single day. For example, now is the first time in human history that, in some countries, nearly anyone can take a convenient DNA test through the mail to check for potential diseases, hereditary traits, and family lineage, or simply in hopes of uncovering hidden family secrets.

Technological and scientific advances have also led to higher standards of living in many parts of the world as our needs continue to be met with greater efficiency and on a wider scale. Meeting our advancing human needs can be seen as a societal challenge, and societal challenges always lead to innovation. In return, innovation leads to solutions and even more change still, creating a constant cycle.

### Innovating for a Higher Purpose

The innovation-change cycle can be illustrated by the work of Abraham Maslow. If you're not familiar with Maslow, he was a twentieth-century American psychologist, best known for developing the concept of Maslow's hierarchy of needs, typically depicted as a pyramid consisting of five levels that address our material and immaterial human needs.

At the bottom level, we have our most basic physiological needs, such as food, shelter, and clothing. The next level up is safety, covering aspects like personal safety and financial security. Level three is that of friendship, family, and a sense of connection, known as the love and belonging level. The fourth level is esteem, including self-esteem, status, and the feeling of accomplishment. And the top level is self-actualization, basically a level that's all about being the best people we can be, focused on a sense of morality, personal development, and creativity.

This pyramid shows that as one set of needs are met, others arise, and they always will until we reach the self-actualization zone. And though self-actualization is an excellent concept we should all strive for, it seems that for most people, more material desires will continue to replace any that have been met. (I'll leave whether or not this is an endless cycle to the psychologists and real therapists.) The point is that, depending on time, place, and circumstances, fulfilling all of these needs presents challenges, especially as we move on up the pyramid.

Maslow's hierarchy can actually be seen as one of innovation in practice. Innovation solves the issues society faces at each level, meeting demands of our physical safety, human collaboration, and social, cultural, and economic change. It's a forward-looking mindset and attitude, and it can't exist on its own, but only in relation to the world around us.

This concept can be illustrated by observing the earth at night. In 2017, NASA scientists released new global maps of the earth after the sun goes down around the world.[32] Produced almost every decade for the past twenty-five years, these "night light" maps contribute to a better understanding of our world, including changing economic, social, and environmental implications. When looking at the map, the first thing that jumps out is how dark it actually is throughout much of the globe despite a number of bright clusters. The dark areas are mostly spread out in developing countries, many of which have yet to begin experiencing the effects of the Fourth Industrial Revolution.

While some of us are living in smart houses, with amenities like connected irrigation systems, and are sending off cotton swabs of DNA to learn about our personal genomics, almost half of the world has yet to get connected to the Internet.[33] While we're playing on our smartphones, swiping left on Tinder, or watching YouTube videos, one-third of the world population lacks access to clean water[34] and half of the world population doesn't have access to basic healthcare.[35]

I don't make these comparisons to be flip or to embarrass or shame anyone—there's nothing wrong with taking advantage of the Fourth Industrial Revolution's opportunities to pursue a variety of experiences. I bring these issues up because I firmly believe that we all have a responsibility to improve the living conditions for people everywhere. Such improvement can only happen through innovation and economic opportunity. Organizations that are leading this change by investing in making the world a better place end up benefiting more than just their shareholders—they benefit everyone.

### The Rise of Purpose-Driven Businesses

Thanks to a younger generation's increasing focus on greater purpose in their work besides income, social and environmental concerns have come to play a pivotal role in the Fourth Industrial Revolution. As we move higher on Maslow's pyramid, we are no longer just trying to improve life conditions for ourselves, but to ensure a better life for all, not to mention the planet's survival. Thanks to globalization and hyper-connectivity, the environments in which many organizations exist have shifted from local to regional to global, meaning that their products and services, as well as actions and values, can now affect people all over the world.

We are witnessing the emergence of companies that are as passionate about social impact as they are about profits. These "benefit corporations," which are popping up in the US and all over the rest of the world, are for-profit companies that produce a social or public benefit. While this definition could hypothetically be applied to a vast array of companies, those that receive Benefit Corporation designation must first meet a number of requirements, based around their impact on their community, customers, employees, and the environment.

Globally, this is turning into what's called the "B-corp" movement, with purpose-driven companies aimed at creating benefits for all stakeholders—direct and indirect—not simply shareholders. As of 2019, there were more than 2,700 certified B-corp companies across 64 countries and 150 industries.[36] These companies range from household names like Kickstarter and Patagonia to others such as Animikii in Canada, a web services company owned and operated by indigenous people working to develop better economic and social outcomes for indigenous communities, and Brazil's Natura Cosméticos SA, a publicly traded multinational worth $3 billion that has more than 2 million employees and advocates for the Amazon forest and produces carbon-neutral products.[37]

Many of the technological, economic, and societal changes that are taking place today are truly earth-shattering, but as with everything else under the sun, they're also somewhat temporary—there's already talk of a fifth Industrial Revolution right around the bend. There's no certainty about when it will begin or how it will evolve, but one thing is for sure: it will require innovation as the most crucial element for success. This is why we must always seek to understand the environment in which we live and how it's changing. The world's most competitive organizations, cities, and even countries have had one thing in common—they were able to anticipate and shape what's next, while delivering value to themselves and their stakeholders. The writing is always on the wall, but if we don't read it and act upon it, then it's not going to do us any good.

## Know When to Take Action

I often work with people who try to wait for the stars to align in perfect formation before taking action on a project or initiative. They feel as if everything must be just right or else there's no reason to begin. While the expression "timing is everything" is somewhat true, there will never be *perfect* alignment. Instead of waiting for perfection, we must have the confidence to execute, even if a few components are less than certain. Considering how fast the world moves today, we can't sit on our hands and wait for everything to line up, because this will never happen—things are in constant motion. Urgency is real, and it defines what an organization does both right now and in the future. With the rate of change today, delay and hesitance are our worst enemies as climatic shifts can take place in the blink of an eye.

In this rapidly changing world, always being prepared to work with the next shift is the new norm. We can't procrastinate or "put innovation off" for a rainy day. Innovation is a constant transformation, a fluid state—and it needs to be nurtured to succeed. There's a significant danger in thinking you've "completed transformation" into an "innovative company," as if it's a one-time, singular event or something that only takes place when change is afoot (then again, if you've been reading closely, you know change is always afoot). This flawed view of what innovation is and how it works can lead to stagnation, just as success can.

As Andy Grove, former CEO of Intel famously said, "Success breeds complacency. Complacency breeds failure. Only the paranoid survive."[38] We don't want future generations looking back in the rearview mirror at all these changes—which will be slow paced to them—and see us sitting there twiddling our thumbs. What's happening now will one day seem like one archaic system that was replaced by another archaic system, just as those from a couple of centuries ago look archaic to us.

For example, most people were far from thrilled about cars when they first became available to the public. States passed all sorts of laws to impede their progress, including Vermont, which required that someone walk in front of a moving car while waving a red flag.[39] If you think gridlock is bad now in some of the world's biggest cities, imagine if every car needed a person to usher it through the streets. Other cities took an even more radical approach and banned cars altogether. Then there were groups like the Farmers' Anti-Automobile Society of Pennsylvania that suggested state laws involving an elaborate system of sending up roman candle rockets as cars drove through the night, whose drivers were also supposed to pull over and cover their cars in blankets or some type of camouflage when passing horses in an effort not to spook them.[40] I don't think any of those made it into law.

It's funny now, but who knows what people will be laughing at in the future, considering our current era as just another quaint time period. Commuter drones, for example, are already being developed by Boeing and Airbus, and dozens of other companies are joining the competition.[41] Someday soon, you may see your next-door neighbors seamlessly carpooling together on drones while you're stuck in traffic, puttering along the highway, late to work. Sounds hard to believe? Take it from Henry Ford, who all the way back in 1940 said, "Mark my words. A combination of airplane and motorcar is coming. You may smile. But it will come."[42]

For leaders and managers, part of the job description must now be to relentlessly communicate today's urgency across all functions in the organization. You must be radically transparent with everyone, including yourself, about the challenges and opportunities of the Fourth Industrial Revolution, and how your organization is affected by it. No matter if you are a board member, top executive, middle manager, or shift supervisor, it is your job to get everyone on your team to pay attention and take change seriously. Whenever you have an audience—whether it's your boss, a bureaucratic committee of some kind, or the entire employee community—you must reiterate that no one can afford to continue the status quo, regardless of how comfortable that is.

Consistently showing your teams that you are serious about innovation will have a tremendous impact on your organization, but proving that it's necessary for survival will be even stronger. Managers and leaders should be measured on ensuring that innovation is seen as a constant priority throughout the organization. In doing so, their companies will remain relevant and meet today's, and the future's, opportunities and challenges.

## Case Study: LEGO

My five-year-old son Matthew is crazy about his LEGOs. I find them all over the house—the living room, his bedroom, the kitchen, the bathroom (specifically the bathtub, which came with a $90 bill from a plumber)—there seems to be an endless supply. Matthew's favorite pastime is to put them together in all sorts of shapes with my wife, Maria. Needless to say, LEGOs are high on my personal radar, mostly as walking hazards covering the floor. But there's another reason I'm interested in them. LEGO is a great example of a company that intimately understands that innovation is always constant, urgent, and time-sensitive.

It may seem ironic that with all this talk of the technological advances of the Fourth Industrial Revolution and the changing world around us, LEGO—whose flagship interlocking plastic bricks began production in 1949—is a prime example of these principles. Before you jump to conclusions, consider that children around the world spend 5 billion hours a year playing with LEGO bricks.[43] Since 1949, more than 400 billion of these bricks have been produced. As for their minifigures, they sell 3.9 of them per second, every day of the year. That adds up to over 122 million of these little guys and girls annually. If that doesn't pique your interest, then this will: in 2018, in opposition of toy industry trends, LEGO increased its market share in all major markets, with its revenue growing 4 percent to around $5.5 billion.[44] Oh, and Ryan of Ryan ToysReview reportedly loves LEGOs as well.[45] Coincidence?

In 2003, with LEGO on the verge of bankruptcy, no one would have guessed that the company would be reporting such strong earnings or be dubbed "the Apple of toys" sixteen years later.[46] Facing major competition in the 1990s from a new wave of video games and computers, paired with shrinking independent toy stores around the world, LEGO took the "ignore it" approach, hiding behind a false confidence in what the company termed its "classic market" position and failing to take action or even admit that the industry was being disrupted.[47]

In time, leaders across LEGO started to realize that if they wanted the company, and their jobs, to survive, a new approach was necessary. As Christian Majgaard, a former LEGO executive and Head of Global Brand and Business Development put it, "We said, 'We want to be the world's most powerful brand among families and children.' That's the new starting point."[48] They set off on a path of open innovation, engaging their customers unlike ever before. The R&D Future Lab team was established and tasked with developing low-risk, low-cost minimum viable prototypes that could quickly be created and tested. Contrary to the way typical companies work, the team shared early prototypes with customers and pivoted based on the feedback, before making any substantial investments in new products.

Most importantly, R&D co-innovated with their end customers through an online platform where consumers were encouraged to share, and vote for, additions to the company's product line. This feedback created a more customer-centric experience, up-to-date with current trends, and resulted in new lines such as LEGO Architecture, popular with adults, and LEGO friends, which turned out to be one of LEGO's biggest successes in the company's history.[49]

The company also began developing partnerships and strategic alliances with Hollywood movie companies. Where Star Wars action figures were once a competitor, they now had their own line. Taking a more holistic view of what their customers wanted, and what LEGO could become, they started opening amusement parks and exhibitions. These were big, bold steps, but even seemingly small changes like a more user-friendly website contributed to their success.

They were forced into action to innovate once, but since then they've respected the urgency and continuity of innovation almost as the word of law. Open innovation has become the party line at LEGO. The Future Lab is now focused on even more forward-looking initiatives, tasked with inventing new, technologically enhanced "play experiences" around the world.[50] They've made inroads into China, partnering with the Tencent Internet company, creating opportunities to experiment with digital technologies and a growing consumer base. They're still producing and selling their iconic blocks, but they're also trying out mobile apps and playing with the integration of physical toys and the digital world. Sounds pretty Fourth Industrial Revolution, no?

## Summary: Innovation Waits for No One

If innovation is not top of mind, then you're going to be left behind. Today's unicorns can easily become tomorrow's Blockbusters, but such a fate only awaits those companies that refuse to remain relevant. As markets continue to change even more rapidly through new technological and scientific advancements, the global social, economic, and business environment will quickly evolve as well. New demands require new responses, and challenges unique to the Fourth Industrial Revolution will surely be solved through continuous change, paving the way for the fifth revolution, sixth revolution, and so on. At the end of the day, one of the only things in this world that is permanent is change—the other is innovation.

It's no secret that companies die, nor is it a secret as to why. As in the past, future progress can only be enabled through innovation, and businesses must take this sentiment to heart or face the consequences. It doesn't matter what the excuse is for inaction; failure to act for any reason will produce the same negative results time and time again. That's why a sense of urgency and duty must be instilled throughout your organization—from employee to middle manager to the CEO and the board. Still, truly embracing change and innovation may be difficult, especially if innovation has never truly been prioritized or has fallen by the wayside. Since that's the case, there must be a leader in place to develop and drive strategies—the topic of Chapter 2.

### Principle

The only thing that is constant is change. Innovation is urgent, time sensitive, and always present.

### Action

- Pay attention to current social, economic, and technological transformations that may be affecting your organization and understand their implications.

- Communicate the urgency of innovation to meet the challenges of change throughout the organization.

### Obstacle

A rapidly changing world means we must get educated and get out of our comfort zone, but many of us remain resistant to change, even when it's staring us right in the face, and do everything to maintain the status quo.

### Outcome

Leaders and employees are attentive to social, technological, and business changes and are willing to embrace them.

## Notes

1. Scott D. Anthony, S. Patrick Viguerie, Evan I. Schwartz, and John Van Landeghem, "2018 Corporate Longevity Forecast: Creative Destruction Is Accelerating," *Innosight Executive Briefing*, February 2018, https://www.innosight.com/wp-content/uploads/2017/11/Innosight-Corporate-Longevity-2018.pdf.
2. CB Insights, "$1B+ Market Map: The World's 326 Unicorn Companies in One Infographic," *CB Insights Research Briefs*, March, 14, 2019, https://www.cbinsights.com/research/unicorn-startup-market-map/.
3. Ibid.
4. Punit Renjen, "The Fourth Industrial Revolution Will Change the World—but Only 14% of Execs Are Ready for It," *World Economic Forum*, January 12, 2018, https://www.weforum.org/agenda/2018/01/87-of-ceos-say-the-fourth-industrial-revolution-will-improve-equality-but-are-they-ready-for-it/.

5. Marketdata LLC, "The U.S. Weight Loss & Diet Control Market," Research and Markets, February 2019, https://www.researchandmarkets.com/research/qm2gts/the_72_billion?w=4.

6. Abigail Hess, "The 10 Most Educated Countries in the World," CNBC.com, February 7, 2018, https://www.cnbc.com/2018/02/07/the-10-most-educated-countries-in-the-world.html.

7. Felix Gussone, MD, "America's Obesity Epidemic Reaches Record High, New Report Says," *NBCNews.com*, October 13, 2017, https://www.nbcnews.com/health/health-news/america-s-obesity-epidemic-reaches-record-high-new-report-says-n810231.

8. Ibid.

9. Jon Porter, "The Last Blockbuster in America Is Now the Last in the World," *The Verge*, May 7, 2019, https://www.theverge.com/2019/3/7/18254381/last-blockbuster-usa-world-australia-closing.

10. Rick Munarriz, "Blockbuster CEO Has Answers," *Motley Fool*, December 10, 2008, https://www.fool.com/investing/general/2008/12/10/blockbuster-ceo-has-answers.aspx.

11. Jon Brodkin, "Myspace Apparently Lost 12 Years' Worth of Music, and Almost No One Noticed," ArtsTechnica.com, March 18, 2019, https://arstechnica.com/information-technology/2019/03/myspace-apparently-lost-12-years-worth-of-music-and-almost-no-one-noticed/.

12. Pamela N. Danziger, "Retail Downsizing Will Accelerate, With UBS Predicting 75,000 Stores Will Be Forced to Close By 2026," *Forbes*, April 10, 2019, https://www.forbes.com/sites/pamdanziger/2019/04/10/retail-downsizing-will-accelerate-as-75000-stores-will-be-forced-to-close-by-2026/#16dc390d339e.

13. PBS, "The Devil's Music: 1920s Jazz," PBS.org, *Culture Shock: The TV Series & Beyond*, 2000, https://www.pbs.org/wgbh/cultureshock/beyond/jazz.html.

14. Ibid.

15. Buddy Iahn, "Kenny G Celebrates 75 Million Albums Sold," *Music Universe*, October 28, 2016, https://themusicuniverse.com/kenny-g-celebrates-75-million-albums-sold/.

16. Connie Johnson, "Kenny G's Hit Broke All the Rules," *LA Times*, June 12, 1987, https://www.latimes.com/archives/la-xpm-1987–06–12-ca-4021-story.html.

17. Ibid.

18. Electronic Frontier Foundation, "RIAA v. The People: Four Years Later," EFF.org, 2007, https://www.eff.org/files/filenode/riaa_at_four.pdf.

19. James Dator, "The Overwatch League Claims Higher Ratings than 'Thursday Night Football . . . but It's Complicated," January 18, 2018, https://www.sbnation.com/lookit/2018/1/18/16905420/overwatch-league-ratings-nfl-thursday-night-football.

20. Ibid.

21. Syracuse Staff, "With Viewership and Revenue Booming, Esports Set to Compete with Traditional Sports," *Syracuse Online Business: Blog*, January 18, 2019, https://onlinebusiness.syr.edu/blog/esports-to-compete-with-traditional-sports/.

22. Sean Campbell, "Overwatch League Shows Esports Marketing Works," *Venture Beat*, May 14, 2019. https://venturebeat.com/2019/05/14/overwatch-league-shows-esports-marketing-works/.

23. Natalie Robehmed and Madeline Berg, "Highest-Paid YouTube Stars 2018: Makipier, Jake Paul, PewDiePie and More," *Forbes*, December 3, 2018, https://www.forbes.com/sites/natalierobehmed/2018/12/03/highest-paid-youtube-stars-2018-markiplier-jake-paul-pewdiepie-and-more/#29cf3029909a.

24. Technology Intelligence, "Worst Tech Predictions of All Time," *Telegraph*, June 29, 2016, https://www.telegraph.co.uk/technology/0/worst-tech-predictions-of-all-time/youtube-founders/.

25. Ben Gilbert, "YouTube Now Has Over 1.8 Billion Users Every Month, within Spitting Distance of Facebook's 2 billion," *Business Insider*, May 4, 2018, https://www.businessinsider.com/youtube-user-statistics-2018–5.

26. Cisco, "Cisco Visual Networking Index: Forecast and Trends, 2017–2022 White Paper," Cisco: White Papers, February 27, 2019, https://www.cisco.com/c/en/us/solutions/collateral/service-provider/visual-networking-index-vni/white-paper-c11–741490.html.

27. Ibid.

28. Jeff Desjardins, "What Happens in an Internet Minute in 2019?" *Visual Capitalist*, March 13, 2019, https://www.visualcapitalist.com/what-happens-in-an-internet-minute-in-2019/.

29. Simon Torrance and Felix Staeritz, "Is Your Business Model Fit for the Fourth Industrial Revolution?" World Economic Forum, January 15, 2019, https://www.weforum.org/agenda/2019/01/is-your-business-model-fit-for-the-fourth-industrial-revolution/.

30. Ibid.

31. Andy Klein, "Hard Drive Cost Per Gigabyte," *Black Blaze*, July 11, 2017, https://www.backblaze.com/blog/hard-drive-cost-per-gigabyte/.

32. NASA, "New Night Light Maps Open Up Possible Real-Time Applications," NASA.gov, April 12, 2017, https://www.nasa.gov/feature/goddard/2017/new-night-lights-maps-open-up-possible-real-time-applications.

33. ITU News, "New ITU Statistics Show More than Half the World Is Now Using the Internet," *ITU News*, December 6,

2018, https://news.itu.int/itu-statistics-leaving-no-one-offline/.

34. WaterAid, "Facts and Statistics," Wateraid.org, 2019, https://www.wateraid.org/facts-and-statistics.
35. World Health Organization, "World Bank and WHO: Half the World Lacks Access to Essential Health Services, 100 Million Still Pushed into Extreme Poverty because of Health Expenses," *WHO.int*, December 13, 2017, https://www.worldbank.org/en/news/press-release/2017/12/13/world-bank-who-half-world-lacks-access-to-essential-health-services-100-million-still-pushed-into-extreme-poverty-because-of-health-expenses.
36. Certified B Corporation, "A Global Community of Leaders," bcorporation.net, 2019, https://bcorporation.net/.
37. Ibid.
38. Andy Grove, *Only the Paranoid Survive: How to Exploit the Crisis Points that Challenge Every Company* (New York: Crown Business, 1999).
39. Martin Schneider, "100 Years Ago, Some People Were Really Hostile to the Introduction of the Automobile," *Dangerous Minds*, November 17, 2013, https://dangerousminds.net/comments/100_years_ago_some_people_were_really_hostile_to_the_introduction.
40. Ibid.
41. Michelle Toh and Jon Ostrower, "People Are Now Flying Around in Autonomous Drones," *CNN Business*, February 18, 2018, https://money.cnn.com/2018/02/08/technology/ehang-self-flying-drone/index.html.
42. Robin Lineberger, Aijaz Hussain, Siddhant Mehra, and Derek M. Pankratz, "Elevating the Future of Mobility: Passenger Drones and Flying Cars," Deloitte Insights, 2019, https://www2.deloitte.com/insights/us/en/focus/future-of-mobility/passenger-drones-flying-cars.html.

43. Julie Stern, "LEGO Fun Facts," LEGO: Background Information, 2009, https://www.planitnorthwest.com/shopping/pdfs/legolandfunfacts.pdf.
44. LEGO, "The LEGO Group Returns to Growth in 2018," LEGO Newsroom, February 27, 2019, https://www.lego.com/en-us/aboutus/news-room/2019/february/annual-results-2018.
45. Robehmed and Berg, "Highest-Paid YouTube Stars 2018."
46. Jonathan Ringen, "How Lego Became the Apple of Toys," *Fast Company*, January 8, 2015, https://www.fastcompany.com/3040223/when-it-clicks-it-clicks.
47. Joseph Brookes, "The Innovation and Customer Experience Culture that Lego Says Saved It from Disruption," *Which-50*, February 21, 2019, https://which-50.com/the-innovation-and-customer-experience-culture-that-lego-says-saved-it-from-disruption/.
48. Ibid.
49. Neda Ulaby, "Girls Legos Are A Hit, But Why Do Girls Need Special Legos?" *National Public Radio, "Weekend Edition Saturday,"* June 29, 2013, https://www.npr.org/2013/06/29/196605763/girls-legos-are-a-hit-but-why-do-girls-need-special-legos.
50. Ringen, "How Lego Became the Apple of Toys."

# Chapter 2

## No Leadership = No Strategy = No Innovation

When I think about the most innovative places in the world, Singapore inevitably comes to mind. When Prime Minister Lee Kuan Yew was elected to office in 1959, Singapore was still reeling from the aftereffects of the Second World War. Infrastructure was scant, the GDP was low, and the island city-state's future was none too bright. Yew set out on a five-year plan based around industrialization, urban renewal, public housing, and educational reform.[1] He saw how the country was changing, its citizens fed up and searching for a sense of prosperity that alluded them, and realized a comprehensive, progressive strategy was needed to confront the most pressing issues of the day. In August of 1965, Singapore gained full independence.

Fast forward sixty years, and Singapore is now one of the ten richest countries in the world.[2] It is internationally recognized for its support of innovation and entrepreneurship and it has positioned itself to become the first "Smart Nation," with a focus on seamless technology, new business opportunities in the digital economy, and international partnerships.[3] Where they once manufactured and exported fishing hooks and mosquito-repelling incense, they're now doing so with aerospace, biotech, and semiconductor products.[4] They also host the Association of Southeast

Asian Nations (ASEAN) headquarters of many major companies, including Apple, Cisco, Microsoft, and BMW.[5] As of 2017, the total foreign direct investment (FDI) in Singapore added up to more than $63.6 billion, an increase of 684 times from the FDI of 1970.[6]

Singapore is huge on coordinated research, with the government committing $16 billion between 2011 to 2015 in an effort—that paid off—to establish Singapore as a global R&D hub.[7] An additional $19 billion was committed to research, innovation, and other enterprises from 2016 to 2020.[8] This push included investment in universities, new technologies, manufacturing, healthcare, and urban planning.[9] Singapore's leaders believe in creating an environment in which their citizens can live meaningful, fulfilled lives, "empowered by digital technology, where digital connectivity leads to stronger community bonds, and many more opportunities for Singaporeans to pursue their aspirations and contribute to Singapore's future."[10]

Global competition relies on innovation, and Singapore is proof positive. The country's leadership recognized what needed to be done, taking into account their citizens' needs and desires, and finding ways to fulfill them. Their main strategy focused on attracting foreign investors, beginning with Yew's creation of the Economic Development Board, whose mission today is "to create sustainable economic growth, with vibrant business and good job opportunities for Singapore."[11] This focus led to innovating almost every aspect of Singaporean life. This strategy has helped drive innovation within the country, getting constituents on board with the nation's goals and explaining *why* this smart approach is necessary, both technologically and socially. The government maintains transparency and they engage and enable their citizens. Singapore's leaders understand that success cannot come unless the people are behind them, and in a country where the GDP went from $400 per capita in 1965[12] to over $57,000 in 2019,[13] it's no surprise that they are.

When it comes down to it, innovation is about execution; that's how Singapore got to where it is today—Singapore's leaders didn't just come up with some big ideas and wait around. But execution can't take place without leaders who drive clear strategy by getting others on board. Singapore's leaders, starting with Yew, appealed to human ambitions. In the country's case, it was citizen involvement. In the case of any business, it's employee engagement, which not only keeps employees happy but also connects them with strategy.

Leaders, however, can only connect with employees if they actually know what they care about. Without strong, informed leadership, there is no strategy, and without strategy, there is no innovation. Lack of innovation leads to stagnation. And stagnation? Stagnation leads to death. As a leader, you must take charge to avoid this untimely end. To do so, you need to be open and honest with yourself and your team about where, and why, innovation gets stifled.

## Recognize How Dysfunction and Stagnation Begin

I'd like to be blunt about the company I work for, the company you work for, the companies my neighbors work for, and literally all the others out there: every single one of them (just like any organization) is somewhat dysfunctional. We can try to fool ourselves into thinking that ours is the exception to the rule, but deep in our hearts, we all know the truth—a gap exists between where we are and where we want to be. There are aspects of our jobs that we could all do better; there are initiatives that get lost, ignored, or forgotten. We miss opportunities, and we don't always learn from our failures. And that's normal—we just have to try our best and move forward. If we don't, stagnation is bound to happen. Aside from the obvious fact that we are all human, stagnation and dysfunction take place in our professional environment due to a lack of information sharing, bureaucracy, and subsequent disempowerment and disengagement.

In many organizations, any meaningful and honest information is rarely shared with employees or across management levels. Often, as long as leadership sees favorable metrics, they'll be reluctant to drive change. Many leaders end up being surrounded by "yes-men" and "yes-women," and take their word as gospel for what's happening down in the trenches. After all, employees rarely get promoted for saying no or being too radical. "Yes-people" do well in corporations because employees are trained to say yes. The same situation can be found in almost any highly structured environment—always say yes, don't speak unless you're spoken to, and never skip rank. There's no way innovation mindsets can flourish in such a stringent setting. I had a similar experience growing up in Russia, a society in which you must *never* question your elders—or government, for that matter.

Back at the office, as ideas, proposals, or any other information moves up the ladder, it becomes massaged into compromises and stripped of many important but politically risky particulars. By the time the initiatives reach decision makers' desks, they often lack any true advantage and are almost completely risk-free, telling leaders exactly what they want to hear. As a result, leaders aren't aware of what's going on, especially in regard to new and different ideas that challenge the organizational status quo. If such ideas go unnoticed and unheeded for even a couple years, there will be no incentive for anyone to share them, so employees keep their mouths shut and heads down. Or they'll work on their new ideas, even while they're on the clock, dreaming about the days they'll escape the company and perhaps put it out of business.

Middle management rarely makes the time to share any information with employees either, or, frankly, they don't have access to it in the first place. Information barely flows vertically—forget about horizontally. Horizontally, leaders don't want to rock the boat with their peers and endanger their social relationships. Without freely sharing information, though, no one knows what's going on. If the uppermost levels of the company think everything's fine, then they're unlikely to focus on diversifying or changing their business. With no real incentive for them or the employees downstream to try something new, no effort will be made to develop a proactive growth strategy. Without growth, stagnation prevails.

### High Rates, and the High Cost, of Disengagement

When it seems like no one knows what's going on in an organization, irritation sets in, especially with employees and middle managers who have to deal with the resulting dysfunction. It's no wonder that employee engagement rates are so low. According to a 2019 Gallup poll, 85 percent of employees were either not engaged or were actively disengaged at work.[14] They don't feel empowered to make an impact, and they have little, if any, connection to the company's mission, strategy, or outcomes. Even worse, many employees barely know what the mission is, let alone the strategy or outcomes to achieve it, typically because it is never fully explained or consistently emphasized. Innovation requires *at least* a basic employee awareness of this information. The same goes for the value they are offering their customers. Employees may know the main products and services, but they aren't nearly as familiar with the broad corporate portfolio, competition, or value positioning. Why? Probably because nobody ever shared that information with them. They're stuck not knowing what the business actually is, who the main customers are, or what message the company is trying to get across and for what purpose.

If employees don't feel like they can make an impact or that their work is not valued, then they'll do the same thing they see their leaders do all the time—check out and pretend to stay the course. Even when they believe their leaders are wrong or a project is a dead end, they won't speak up, mostly in deference to their bosses (who, again, might not have a clue as to what's really happening anyhow). Unfortunately, such awkward silence—the deafening kind heard in many staff meetings every day throughout the corporate world—is generally a product of an outdated business culture that only values the word of the highest-paid person's opinion (HiPPO). True innovation means challenging the status quo. To do that, HiPPOs must be challenged too, and they must accept different opinions wholeheartedly. Only once they begin listening to others can they truly connect with and empower others.

When awareness and, as a result, connection to others are priorities, the company's purpose empowers everyone. Take the story of President John F. Kennedy's first visit to NASA headquarters in 1961.[15] As the tale goes, while walking around the office, the president struck up a conversation with a janitor. He politely asked him what he did there at NASA. Most likely expecting a response like "mop the floors, take out the trash, the usual," JFK must have been somewhat taken aback when the janitor looked at him with a smile and replied, "I'm helping put a man on the moon!"[16] Now that's the kind of employee who knows the organizational mission and has a tangible and proud connection to it.

I guarantee that at that time at NASA—which was really just a startup then—there was a leader involved who worked to unite everyone across the organization so they understood what they were striving for. As a result, employees recognized their own contribution and the difference they could actually make in the organization, in the greater world, and even beyond. Think about how many of your employees connect with a bigger picture. Do you yourself know what it is? If not, it's time to get some clarity—you'll need it to drive strategy.

## Take Responsibility

To develop an innovation-driven strategy, leaders need to get their heads out of the sand and into the game. If they don't know what's happening on the floor below or the office next to them, they won't be able to relate to their employees, and surely no one is going to buy in, or even understand what's being said, when it comes to talk of "innovation." "Innovate what?" they'll ask. Unfortunately, very few leaders have an answer to that question. In most cases, neither they, nor their company, nor the individual departments, have any forward-looking strategy when it comes to innovation.

It's not enough to proclaim weak platitudes like "Be innovative," "Dream big," or "Think bold"—let's not confuse corporate propaganda with actual strategy. Normally when leaders cough up such ill-thought-out slogans, they don't actually consider what those words mean. Ask them and many will be stunned into silence before running to the nearest fire escape and sneaking off.

They'd save themselves a lot of trouble, however, if they had a strategy in hand that they could point to.

To that end, when it comes to innovation, leaders across levels and functions must hold themselves responsible for clearly defined pathways, actions, and outcomes. Remember, innovation doesn't happen naturally—so an innovation mindset must be incentivized and supported.

As a leader, that's your job.

### Start with a Goal in Mind

To help innovation thrive, begin by understanding why your business needs it in the first place, and for what purpose. Start big and then home in on the strategy that aligns best with your company's priorities. First, ask what value you can offer your customer, which is more or less corporate speak for "How do we make money while providing a product or service?" From there, think about a general goal related to creating and offering value. When it comes to innovation, any goal can fall under one of four main categories:

- Human aspirations are a key driving factor, and pretty much every innovation throughout history originally resulted from an individual or a group of individuals pursuing their ambitions. When it comes to the business environment, ambition, curiosity, and legacy play a major role in many leaders' plans, decisions, and strategy.
- Survival is the market position you need to retain to remain in business. If your competitors are on top of innovation and you aren't, it's likely that you'll see a negative change in your market share, or your entire market might just go away. As a goal, "just surviving" may not sound all that exciting, but if you remember Maslow's pyramid, basic survival is essential to prosperity and growth.
- Operational efficiency relies on optimizing the processes and costs in an effort to increase the speed of production or time

to market. This goal, and any of its related strategies, has been popularized through lean methods, some to great fanfare.
- Growth requires the greatest attention to the future. Here, your company shapes or creates new markets and increases its footprint and revenues. Ideally, innovation will always lead to growth over time.

These goals do not always come in a particular order and will vary based on the size and state of your organization. If you're a sole proprietor launching a new project, you may have different goals than a well-established corporation whose business model is quickly becoming obsolete. Then again, there are times when even those goals will overlap. Whether you're focusing on one or all four, these goals will develop into strategy. Once you clearly define your mission, purpose, goals, and strategy, a culture of innovation can begin to take hold.

Focus is obviously key to this process—unless you know what you're focused on, you're never going to get anywhere. Think of Alice and the Cheshire Cat in Lewis Carroll's *Alice's Adventures in Wonderland.* When she arrives at a fork in the road, Alice meets a cat who happens to be lounging in a nearby tree. She asks him which way to go, to which the cat sagely replies, "Where do you want to go?" She says she doesn't know. "Then," says the cat, "it doesn't matter." How very true: without a roadmap (a strategy) your destination (the goal) is entirely irrelevant. As a leader, you need to know the destination and develop the roadmap for the journey. You're in charge of your teams' successes and failures, their future and their destinies. Irrespective of where you stand in the organization, it is your responsibility to take the first step in defining innovation goals for them. So, what's the best way to do this? Well, just ask.

## Ask Questions

If you ask employees what innovation means to them and where their company needs to innovate, you might be surprised by their responses. You're likely to find out more than you'd ever expect, including what really matters to them: their concerns, the issues they face in their jobs, their actual opinions about the direction of the company, and, most importantly, what they believe could be improved or radically changed. Innovation requires transparency that only comes about through honest two-way dialogue. If you're not transparent with your employees, the talent market will be *very* transparent with you and you will lose your best people.

Though they may not be getting information from the top, your employees know exactly what's going well, and not so well, on their level, causing them to have valuable insight that no one else can provide. Asking them specific questions will help reveal challenges and opportunities that are prone to innovation in regard to four areas: culture, strategy, companywide execution, and team values. Some questions will be more specific to your company, but try starting with the following list as a template. (And make sure to buckle your seatbelt before you read the responses; what you learn will be priceless.)

## 1. Culture

Do you have meaningful opportunities to share your ideas with leadership and receive feedback?

*Yes / No / Not Sure*

Do you feel your immediate leadership cares about your ideas?

*Yes / No / Not Sure*

Do you have opportunities and resources to implement your ideas?

*Yes / No / Not Sure*

What can we do better to help improve in this area?

________________________________________

________________________________________

(*continued*)

*(continued)*

## 2. Strategy

Do you know what our company's mission and goals are?

*Yes / No / Not Sure*

Do you believe our company has a strategy in place for innovation?

*Yes / No / Not Sure*

Do you understand your team's strategy in relation to achieving your company's mission and goals?

*Yes / No / Not Sure*

What can we do better to help improve in this area?

______________________________________________

______________________________________________

## 3. Companywide Execution

Do you trust our leadership to lead the company forward?

*Yes / No / Not Sure*

Do you think we, as a company, are executing well on our strategy and goals?

*Yes / No / Not Sure*

Are we moving fast enough with our execution?

*Yes / No / Not Sure*

What can we do better to help improve in this area?

______________________________________________

______________________________________________

## 4. Team Values

Can you identify specific things you would change about your team?

*Yes / No / Not Sure*

Do you feel like your team is missing out on opportunities to enact strategy or reach set goals?

*Yes / No / Not Sure*

Do you or your team leaders perform worthless procedures that you feel are unnecessary?

*Yes / No / Not Sure*

What can we do better to help improve in this area?

________________________________________

________________________________________

The answers to these questions will reveal much more than surface-level issues, especially if you avoid the meaningless ambiguity found in survey questions that rely on a nebulous numerical rating scale. If you were to ask your teams about their trust in companywide leadership's decisions on a scale from one to ten—one being they don't trust their leaders and ten being they fully trust their leaders—you're looking at quite a large range of responses to a question that, when push comes to shove, really deserves a yes or no answer. There's also the issue of conformation bias, in which surveys are often worded in a way that will actually support whatever answer you're looking for—which is typically that everything is fine—instead of asking neutral questions that will receive honest answers.

Don't just survey your "star" team members or managers in a particular department either. Talk to *everyone* about each aspect (culture, strategy, companywide execution, team values, and any specifics), regardless of their function. So even though most people would think the sales department would be the official domain to ask, "Which of our products are in the highest demand?" ask your engineering and services teams as well. After all, innovation requires different points of view, and each team brings another, unique perspective.

In the meantime, if you don't already conduct exit polls, you need to start *now.* Your soon-to-be ex-employees are likely to give you the most honest answers during what is typically an emotional conversation—whether one of anger, happiness, sadness, or relief. This is not to say you should exploit their emotions, but you'll probably receive candid opinions that they may have been unwilling to share before. Ask them what they think about the company's culture of innovation, or whether they even think you have one. In an ideal world, their feedback would play an integral role in how leaders help their employees stick to strategy and reach goals. In many ways, the reasons why people leave a company are just as important as why people stay. We rarely quit jobs "just because"—there's always a reason, whether that's a toxic environment, a lack of mobility, a dying industry, or an unwillingness to innovate.

Once you compile feedback from across the company, make sure it doesn't just get saved in the cloud somewhere, only to be stored and ignored. The whole point of asking these questions is to help gain clarity and get a sense of what's happening in the company in order to develop goals and strategy. Remember, you need to define a goal and drive innovation toward it. In advance of your next move, take the time to actually understand what your employees are telling you.

### Before You Act, Shut Up and Listen

As you ask your employees questions and start listening to their responses, you'll undoubtedly get some feedback like "My manager's an idiot" and "I should get paid more," but just remember that many, many people think that their boss is somewhat of a moron and that they deserve higher compensation (some of them are right in both observations, but let's leave that aside for now). Also, it should go without saying that these surveys must remain anonymous to ensure honesty and candor. Since that's the case, you may get some responses that help you take the temperature of the workforce, but don't provide much in the way of prescriptive advice.

Focus instead on the actionable feedback that will lead to concrete goals and the strategy to achieve them. Asking these questions across the board is going to generate a lot of good, hard data on where and how innovation needs to occur. Maybe your employees have suggestions on troubleshooting bottlenecks that are slowing down production. Or maybe they point out initiatives that are floundering and protocols that are time consuming, but ultimately unnecessary. They might highlight the lack of resources they have, but need, to complete projects by set deadlines, or shed light on areas for potential growth that you never considered. They will also give you a glimpse of culture across the company.

If you don't listen to those responses and internalize that data, then what was the point of asking in the first place? Don't just assume that you know what's going on. If you give people the chance, they will tell you what they think. Your people know what's important, so if you button it up for a minute and pay attention, you'll make some smart decisions on what to prioritize. Too many leaders fall into the "everything is important" trap, but by that logic nothing is actually important. By identifying priorities, you can clearly outline the goals, which is especially imperative in big companies where a lot of people are involved. Just as "everything" cannot be important, neither can "everything" be within a given goal. Many leaders go for ambiguous goals because they're afraid of narrowing in on a decision and making the wrong bet. Yet this ambiguity is a problem: ambiguity is a death sentence when it comes to innovation, because it's another path toward stagnation. Innovation cannot happen without focus on a goal and set strategy.

Historically, companies rarely listened to their employees because, frankly, they thought employees were disposable. "Who cares if employees quit? We can always hire more." Sadly, there are still some companies with that mentality, but most leaders now understand that there is always institutional knowledge that disappears with exiting employees, whether they are top performers or not. There's also growing competition over talent throughout industries. Any organization that exists today should be all about the people who work there; after all, organizations are built of people, just as our ideas come from people and are developed for people.

The employee experience is therefore vital, so we must listen to employees and take their feedback seriously. Such an environment will only further support company goals and contribute to employees' willingness to work with leaders in driving strategy. You'll get a serious reality check from your employees, and their support and input are essential, but, as a leader, together with your peers, you're still the one who's going to make the final decisions on what goals to strive for and how to get there. To do so, the strategy needs to be crystal clear.

## Clarify and Publish Employee Sentiments, Goals, and Strategy

Your success in developing goals and implementing strategy rides on transparency, which will contribute to nurturing a true relationship with your employees. This connection will increase your ability to lead innovation and growth, or another goal you may have identified. To that end, you must organize and publish the data you've collected—all the employee responses, insights, and suggestions—back to all of the employees themselves. Regretfully, most managers fail to take this approach, typically for three reasons: First, they don't care about their employees' opinions and don't value them. Second, they don't want to hear the truth, as it will require them to take accountability and action. And third, they are somewhat disengaged as well and don't care about what is going on inside the office.

By stepping up and being transparent, we show our employees that we take their opinions seriously, drawing a direct connection between their feedback and strategy, while furthering their empowerment and engagement (and making our jobs a whole hell of a lot easier). When you prove that you are driving accountability in addition to strategy, you begin changing your company's culture for the better. When employees aren't engaged, they feel alone and hopeless. Misery loves company, which means a storm of low morale, but when employees find that their colleagues share their values, have the same concerns, and have identified similar problems, they realize there are opportunities to partner together and create better results. Transparency and a willingness to listen, coupled with self-accountability and guidance, will go a long way to connecting your teams with the goals and strategy developed.

Don't get too fancy or try to make anything sound more complex than it needs to be. Use simple, step-by-step goals and actionable terms. Stating "We aim to disrupt the marketplace by proving unprecedented value for our customers through cutting-edge, innovative initiatives" means absolutely nothing when it comes to a real plan. However, "We aim to increase customer retention by at least 10 percent in Q1, as compared to the previous quarter, through rolling out loyalty programs to 20 percent of our current clients" holds more weight.

Remember, publishing your clear strategy is just the first step—you still have to execute it, and you will surely pivot with time. But taking accountability and spreading awareness is where it all begins. Your entire team needs to feel that you're listening to them and supporting them, and that the goals and strategy you set are implemented with their ideas in mind. Even though no leadership equals no strategy equals no innovation, without employees there's no one to lead. Without employees, you've got nothing.

## Case Study: Wikimedia Foundation

After 244 years, *Encyclopaedia Britannica* published its final physical edition in 2010.[17] The once sought-after, authoritative multi-volume set—used as a source of information, sign of distinction, and piece of home decor—decided it was time to call it quits on print and focus on the online, digital space that had quickly come to displace the reference book industry. There was also a new kid on the block that quietly began ten years earlier to little fanfare, but has since become one of the world's most visited websites.[18] That's right—Wikipedia.

*(continued)*

## Case Study: Wikimedia Foundation (*continued*)

Now hosted and run by the nonprofit Wikimedia Foundation, Wikipedia began as an outgrowth of what was initially called Nupedia, which the creators had envisioned as a comprehensive online encyclopedia, but it was slow to start. The original focus was on the traditional peer review model, with articles written by experts in their fields. After realizing they could only produce about a dozen pieces per year in this manner, co-founders Jimmy Wales and Larry Sanger decided to take another approach—crowdsourcing.

Wikipedia doesn't sell ads, so they're not beholden to any corporate sponsors. Instead, Wales created the Wikimedia Foundation, which now has a major endowment and receives funding from the public, with an average individual donation of $15.86.[19] With a mission to "Empower and engage people around the world to collect and develop educational content under a free license or in the public domain, and to disseminate it effectively and globally,"[20] the organization is clear about its purpose and goals.

But 2010 wasn't the greatest year for Wikipedia either. As *Encyclopaedia Britannica* waved goodbye to print, Wikipedia's contributions were slowing and the numbers of active editors they had crowdsourced over the past decade were declining.[21] Wikimedia was still a tiny nonprofit, with a small staff and budget. It was obvious that they needed to make a change. So who did they turn to for answers? The people who would really know what was going on: their community of editors and writers.

They decided to take a rollcall and found that of their 100,000 active editors at the time, four out of five were male, half of them were under 22 years old, and a vast majority of the edits came from the global north.[22] These were some major red flags—a lack of diverse and global perspectives was the exact opposite of Wikipedia's mission. Unlike many companies or organizations that would sweep this information under the rug, Wikimedia published these findings and then asked their community for suggestions on how to make Wikipedia better. The leaders at that time, including the executive director of Wikimedia, Sue Gardner, set out on a five-year strategic planning project. Over 1,000 people provided them with input in the form of proposals and feedback to tackle the Wikipedia community's challenges and identify what areas to prioritize.[23]

Foundation leaders and facilitators helped synthesize all of the information coming in, while also making it public online for everyone to see, no matter if they were part of the effort, a member of the Wikimedia Foundation, or just some curious bystander. Different groups formed around certain issues, producing even more useable data and suggestions. All of these steps were taken with transparency, community involvement, and a willingness for leaders to listen to what was happening around them, looking into areas that they had previously been blind to. And the endeavor paid off.

Today, Wikipedia features over 48 million articles in hundreds of languages, which would fit into about 19,000 print volumes of *Britannica*.[24] They're widely considered a reputable source of information, with standards of checks and balances in place and a diverse group of volunteer writers. As British journalist Madhumita Murgia stated in 2016, "Wikipedia has become arguably the largest collaborative effort in the history of mankind."[25] And that's all thanks to leaders willing to listen to their teams, developing strategy with their insights and feedback, and driving it forward. It could be argued that Wikipedia is one of the largest *innovative* efforts in history as well, but even if you think that's an exaggeration, I'm sure we can agree it's certainly one for the books.

## Summary: Lead, Strategize, Innovate

No matter how dysfunctional we all are, there's always a way to develop strategy that supports positive change. The process starts with an informed leadership, both middle managers and upper management, willing to risk some of their political capital. As a leader, you must step up and put in the time to uncover what areas throughout your organization are prime for innovation—big or small. Through this process, define what innovation in action looks like within your environment and create an actionable plan for your team.

Ask employees honest, in-depth questions across all functions. Gather responses, publish the data back to everyone in the organization, and get your peers and employees on the same page. Though employees don't develop strategy—remember, that's the leader's job—their input will make it vastly better, and they will be more invested in the results. From there, strategy must be kept alive and in check with marketplace realities to ensure innovation is always present. To do so, leaders need to take accountability for the execution of strategy, enabling their teams' success through the appropriate resources, attention, and care. Still, your strategy could become a recipe for disaster without follow-through and metrics that prove your innovation efforts are effective—the focus of Chapter 3.

### Principle

Strong, dedicated leadership leads to actionable strategy, which is necessary for innovation. No leadership means no strategy, and without either, innovation will shrivel and die on the vine.

### Actions

- Constantly take the pulse of the organization to understand what is working well and what needs to change, while being transparent with the workforce about the results.
- Develop a clear, step-by-step strategy with employee input and make sure it's understood throughout the organization.
- Take accountability for the execution of the strategy throughout the company.

### Obstacles

Political risks and an unwillingness to change the status quo create stagnation. A lack of knowledge, awareness, and engagement by both leaders and employees only contributes to the situation further. Getting everyone involved and focused on attaining a common goal is nearly impossible without clarity and transparency, neither of which are prioritized in most organizations.

### Outcome

Creation of an actionable goal and strategy, mapped out in practical terms, that align the company horizontally and vertically, while identifying where innovation is necessary and efforts should be invested.

## Notes


1. Biography.com Editors, "Lee Kuan Yew Biography," *Biography.com*, April 10, 2019, https://www.biography.com/people/lee-kuan-yew-9377339.
2. Focus Economics, "The Richest Countries in the World," *Focus Economics*, 2019, https://www.focus-economics.com/blog/richest-countries-in-the-world.
3. Smart Nation and Digital Government Office, *Smart Nation: The Way Forward*, 2018, https://www.smartnation.sg/docs/default-source/default-document-library/smart-nation-strategy_nov2018.pdf.
4. Clayton Christensen, Efosa Ojomo, and Karen Dillon, "How Investment Made Singapore an Innovation Hub," *Barron's*, February 6, 2019, https://www.barrons.com/amp/articles/how-investment-made-singapore-an-innovation-hub-51549458040.
5. Ibid.
6. Ibid.
7. National Research Foundation, "Research Innovation Enterprise 2020 Plan," NRF.gov, 2019, https://www.nrf.gov.sg/rie2020/.
8. Ibid.
9. Ibid.
10. Ibid.
11. Christensen, Ojomo, and Dillon, "How Investment Made Singapore."
12. Ibid.
13. Focus Economics, "The Richest Countries."
14. Jim Harter, "Dismal Employee Engagement Is a Sign of Global Mismanagement," *Gallup Blog*, 2019, https://www.gallup.com/workplace/231668/dismal-employee-engagement-sign-global-mismanagement.aspx.

15. Tanya Jansen, "JFK and the Janitor: The Importance of Understanding the Why That Is Behind What We Do," *Beqom*, November 26, 2014, https://www.beqom.com/blog/jfk-and-the-janitor.

16. Ibid.

17. Julie Bosman, "After 244 Years, Encyclopaedia Britannica Stops the Presses," *New York Times*, March 13, 2012, https://mediadecoder.blogs.nytimes.com/2012/03/13/after-244-years-encyclopaedia-britannica-stops-the-presses/.

18. SimilarWeb, "Top Websites Ranking," SimilarWeb, 2019, https://www.similarweb.com/top-websites/.

19. Wikimedia Foundation, *Fundraising Report: 2017–2018*, Wikimedia Foundation, https://meta.wikimedia.org/wiki/Fundraising/2017–18_Report.

20. Wikimedia Foundation, "Wikimedia Foundation Mission," *Wikimedia Foundation: About*, 2019, https://wikimediafoundation.org/about/mission/.

21. Chris Grams, Philippe Beaudette, and Eugene Eric Kim, "Strategic Planning the Wikimedia Way: Bottom-Up and Outside-In," Management Innovation eXchange, May 20, 1011, https://www.managementexchange.com/story/strategic-planning-wikimedia-way.

22. Ibid.

23. Ibid.

24. Wikimedia, "List of Wikipedias," *Wikimedia*, 2019, https://meta.wikimedia.org/wiki/List_of_Wikipedias#Grand_Total.

25. Madhumita Murgia, "How Wikipedia Changed the World," *Telegraph*, January 15, 2016, https://www.telegraph.co.uk/technology/wikipedia/12100516/How-Wikipedia-changed-the-world.html.

# Chapter 3

## If You Can't Measure It, You Can't Manage It

Take a minute to relax. In fact, take a few. Sit up straight, breathe in deeply through your nose, and then out through your mouth. Maybe you're reading this book on the plane or in a coffee shop, but don't be embarrassed if anyone hears you. Instead, try to clear your mind of any surrounding distractions. In a moment, put this book aside and close your eyes. Breathe in and out a few more times, focusing on the air traveling through your lungs. Be still. Then, when you're ready, open your eyes and return to this page. Don't worry, I'll wait.

Did you do it? How do you feel? Well my friend, you just took your first step toward the practice of mindfulness meditation, an in-vogue approach to focusing on the here and now, in which we make ourselves fully present in the moment, despite any overwhelming outside pressures or anxieties. It's a proven way to clear your mind, focus, and destress. Ask someone on the street how to measure meditation, however, and you'll likely get some confused looks. But the truth is, it has actual measurable results, not just in everyday well-being but also in workplace performance. A 2016 study by researchers at Case Western Reserve University found that mindfulness not only improves employees' focus, but also their attention and behavior, and their ability to manage stress and work together.[1]

According to the healthcare provider Aetna, in 2015, offering mindfulness meditation and yoga programs—in which more than one-quarter of the company's 50,000 employees participated in at least one class—had tangible results. Participants reported a 19 percent reduction in pain, 20 percent improvement in sleep quality, and a 28 percent reduction in stress levels.[2] Maybe more importantly for all you practical-minded, type-A managers out there focusing on the bottom line, Aetna reported that these employees gained an average of 62 minutes per week of productivity, at an estimated worth of $3,000 per employee per year.[3] If the company could convince all of its workforce to invest in the mindful meditation practice, Aetna could potentially be looking at an additional $150 million per year—not too shabby. Others have taken notice, with the Mayo Clinic, Google, General Mills, and the US Marine Corps instituting mindfulness meditation practices as well.[45]

As digital clutter and noise continues to grow exponentially, I expect such programs and practices will too. Many of us in the US are already addicted to our smartphones—research shows 39 percent of us believe we're using our phones excessively, and on average, US consumers check their phones 52 times a day.[6] Therapist, author, and speaker Esther Perel provides some much-needed, easy-to-follow advice for us techno-junkies: "If the last thing you touch before you sleep and the first thing you touch when you wake is your phone—change it."[7] And I have a feeling that it's only a matter of time until we all listen up and take note; we increasingly need to create opportunities for ourselves and others to disconnect, reenergize, and refocus, at least once in a while.

Those of us who work in Silicon Valley may be more open to the idea of meditation than those of us who work on Wall Street, but whether or not you think it's too new age for your tastes, meditation works. So does innovation. Like meditation, most people believe that innovation is immeasurable, but this couldn't be farther from the truth. Measuring results in any endeavor can certainly be tricky, but the innovation of introducing meditation to the workplace resulted in clear metrics. Innovation can, and must, be measured. In fact, if you can't measure it, then it's probably not innovation at all; it's more likely "fake innovation."

Fake innovation consists of supposedly innovative initiatives that are highly visible but have no discernible results whatsoever. It normally accompanies grandiose wordplay that junks up mission statements or could be spewed out of a random word generator online, chockfull of jargon with a slight nod to the latest flavor of the month. When put into action, these words quickly disappear and nothing gets done, except for an endless "innovation celebration," in which leaders pat themselves on the back, make a nice toast, and acknowledge just how "innovative" and "strategic" they are. Who wouldn't want to have a good party when somebody else is picking up the check for it later on?

True innovation is all about a clear purpose with measurable results. Who cares if you receive a "most innovative company" award but your customers are unhappy and your employees are leaving? That's where real goals and metrics come in. We all need measurements to drive results, hold ourselves accountable, and show the concrete impact of our efforts. And if our actions aren't truly making a difference, then are we even on the right track?

## Get Real About Innovation

Though innovation is a now-or-never prospect, and we all need to focus on fostering an environment in which it is constant, this doesn't mean that *every* aspect of *every* function needs to be innovative *all the time.* Yes, the concept is central to growth, but you can't always innovate everything, nor should you. Think about it: excessive innovation in accounting, for example, is likely to land you in jail and put your company out of business, which, by the way, is exactly what happened to Enron (ironically, a firm that was named one of "America's Most Innovative" companies by *Fortune* magazine for six consecutive years).[8]

When it comes to most organizations, innovation should almost never be undertaken for innovation's sake alone. Your efforts must be geared toward creating an impact that is going to directly affect your business for the better. Whatever actions you take must be relevant to, and improve, your business. As the guy who pretty much invented modern business management, Peter Drucker is famous for his quote "What gets measured gets improved."[9] This statement holds true when it comes to innovation as well. You must first figure out where you want to innovate and with what purpose, and then consider the metrics.

If you can't measure these efforts and show their clear impact, then they're probably not working. Without demonstrable metrics, you won't improve anything, and "innovation" will lose all credibility, becoming just another expensive team building activity or publicity exercise—what I call "innovation theater." No one will be interested in your innovation endeavors, nor should they be, unless you can demonstrate how they relate to a measurable outcome; otherwise, they're simply irrelevant.

I often hear that innovation requires creativity (which is true), and creativity should not be measured; rather it should be allotted plenty of time and a fat budget (which is false). I've met many corporate innovation managers who believe they shouldn't be measured at all, and they complain that they're being judged on "old metrics." They also tend to think that corporate, sales, marketing, legal, or [insert your other favorite function here] "doesn't get it." Perhaps sometimes that's true, but that doesn't mean they shouldn't be held accountable to some reasonable set of metrics.

And come on—we all know that metrics exist; they're out there for any worthwhile endeavor. As mentioned, every real innovation's results can be measured. If we look at meditation again, consider the Headspace app that has been trying to conquer the $1.2 billion meditation market.[10] Some people would laugh at figuring out a way to measure the company's mission to "improve the health and happiness of the world."[11] But the app has been downloaded over 25 million times,[12] and the company had a 2018 valuation of $320 million.[13] Now that's a real measurement, and an impressive one as well.

Or consider the entirely new circus entertainment industry created by Guy Laliberté and Gilles Ste-Croix, two street performers who formed Cirque de Soleil in Montreal in 1984. To most people, the circus industry at the time didn't need any innovation; by all standards, the typical companies in that space, like Ringling Bros. and Barnum & Bailey Circus, were doing just fine. Pitched as "The Greatest Show on Earth," Ringling Bros. got its start in 1871 and was going strong for over a hundred years when Laliberté and Ste-Croix emerged on the scene.[14] Unlike many other entertainers, they saw a space for innovation. They took risks, they made wise moves, and they delivered. And in addition to being amazingly creative, just like any other commercial enterprise, they had a metric too: acceptance by the public and the resulting hundreds of millions of fans, fortune, fame, and the profitability and growth that have followed. In 2017, Ringling Bros. and Barnum & Bailey Circus closed after a 146-year run; in 2016–2017, Cirque du Soleil had an estimated revenue of $791 million, another impressive measurement.[15]

If we can measure the effects of meditation and the performing arts, we should be able to measure just about anything. Your investors—as well as others paying your bills, such as customers, shareholders, taxpayers, bosses, corporate partners, or otherwise—need these real measurements to understand your impact and decide whether to continue supporting you. Telling management that you're "innovative 4.0" and "hyper-collaborative" isn't enough. You need to show them hard evidence of what you're actually doing and how you're making an impact. If you can draw a line of sight for them between innovation and its effects, you'll be lightyears ahead of all the other leaders who briefly mention the word "innovation" in their daily staff meetings. Remember, most senior leaders in non-tech industries are already likely to be skeptical of the concept of "innovation," especially if they find it amorphous. (If they read this book, I hope they'll see that innovation doesn't fall under that category, but hey, your boss may not be so enlightened yet.) They want to see proof; they want to see the metrics.

And that's okay. No matter what role we play in a company—from the first-year assistant to the seasoned CEO—we're all measured, as we should be. We need to be judged on our achievements, performance, and ability to execute in partnership with others so we know what actually creates results and how we can improve ourselves. If we don't see results over a reasonable amount of time, then we're most likely doing something wrong and have to change course. Through measurement, we drive outcomes and highlight the direct link between a potentially intangible concept and concrete results. If innovation is driving impact, one way or another, there's certainly a metric to prove it; you just need to find the right one.

## Find the Metrics

Here's the deal: in the mindfulness meditation example, metrics such as reduction in levels of pain and stress and an increase in the quality of sleep are important, but these are somewhat soft metrics. The underlying key metric is improved performance, which leads to—you guessed it—increased revenue for the company. Headspace has certainly helped a lot of people in their personal and professional lives, including myself, but the hard metrics of their business success is that $320 million valuation. And yes, Cirque du Soleil graduated from being a colorful group of characters roaming the streets of Canada to being adored by fans internationally, but if we want to talk hard metrics, they created new value and became the largest theatrical production company in the world, with earnings moving toward $1 billion per year. So although there are plenty of ways to measure innovation's effects, when all is said and done, in a business environment, those effects must contribute to increased revenue.

Don't muddy the waters by trying to come up with "new measurements" for innovation. Stay away from complex balanced scorecards that rely on some mysterious average score. Unfortunately, I often see these meaningless metrics pop up, where an entire team spent months developing a very complicated (and probably expensive) system to rate innovation. You'll hear the term "innovation index" paraded around, but when you inspect the numbers they often don't show any useful and actionable information. If you try to create such a system and present the results, most of your stakeholders will end up arguing about your methodology, rather than focusing on your successes, or what you need to reach those successes.

Instead, focus on how you can impact some other already existing metrics. I'm referring to the classics here, which generally fall into two categories: activity metrics and impact metrics. I sat down with Scott Kirsner of Innovation Leader to discuss these metrics and their relation to innovation. Innovation Leader is an unbiased, independent media and events company and Scott, who is the CEO and co-founder, is pretty much the authority in the world of innovation, particularly when it comes down to changing the behavior in large organizations. (Full disclosure: I'm a member of Innovation Leader's editorial board.) Scott and I talked about the challenging world of measuring innovation, particularly the activity and impact metrics, which the company has also outlined in its various research.[16]

Activity metrics highlight your actions, or how "busy" your team's been. In this category, Scott and Innovation Leader include "patent applications or patents granted; employees trained in an innovation method; ideas collected, researched, or prototyped; [and] startup companies you've met with or established partnerships with."[17] Other activity metrics they refer to are "speeches given at innovation conferences or times your projects have been mentioned in the press; demand from throughout the company for consulting or services from the innovation team; seed funding grants you've given to employee projects; or academic collaborations."[18]

For example, conducting the survey from Chapter 2, tallying the results, and publishing the data are all activity metrics. Aetna offering a meditation and yoga program is an activity metric as well. Any activities you've performed in developing and refining your innovation strategy and executing toward a goal falls under this category.

Impact metrics, on the other hand, are those that show the tangible results of these activities. Scott explained that revenue is the main impact metric, but it's not the only one. As described in an Innovation Leader report, impact metrics can also include the following: "Products or services incubated by an innovation team may expand a company's shelf space or distribution footprint. They may establish a presence in a new customer segment or a geographic market that matters to the company."[19] These products and services may also "boost customer loyalty, or Net Promoter Score. . . . They may open up a new business model—like adding service revenue to a company that previously sold only products, or vice versa. They may reduce costs."[20]

Expanding Cirque du Soleil to many cities in the world would be an activity metric, and the $791 million they pulled down in one year is an impact metric. When it comes to innovation, impact metrics are broader than just revenue, such as a reduction in operating cost or, in Aetna's case, the increased productivity of $3,000 per year, per employee who participated in the meditation and yoga program. Still, I always recommend focusing on two tried-and-true impact metrics: revenue generated from innovation process improvements, products, and services, and savings generated from innovation process improvements, products, and services.

Activity metrics and impact metrics are both important—one can't happen without the other—but most executives disproportionately focus on activity over impact, at least initially. This emphasis causes innovation leaders to get wrapped up in the activity metrics as well, making a big show of innovation in an effort to get others excited and involved, and to appease their bosses as well. However, when the numbers come in at the end of the quarter or the company is hit with a budget crunch, if innovation leaders can't prove that they've made an impact, they're the first to be shown the door.

There is an inherent Catch-22 in any innovation effort when it comes to these metrics—there will always be a time lapse between an activity and its impact. The corporate world is especially impatient when it comes to results, often supporting a "current quarter" mentality. So even if executives like seeing a flurry of activity, they do have an expectation that it will be converted into impact metrics, and quickly. If it's not, then any focus on innovation might be lost as management gives up and moves on. Balancing activity and impact is probably the hardest part for any innovation manager and a frequent topic over drinks at industry conferences. To be successful, it's essential that you maintain a careful balance between activity metrics and impact metrics, never losing sight of your goal. That means you must be careful about the metrics you pick to showcase innovation.

In addition to the metrics you choose, make sure that you are tracking those that are specifically related to your strategy and goals. Since you're most likely working with a variety of stakeholders, it's also important to identify who is looking at these metrics and what you are trying to demonstrate that is of relevance to them. Keep in mind that many factors contribute to results, not just innovation, so avoid the temptation to double count or otherwise stretch the truth when measuring and communicating the impact of innovation. The best way to track and reveal convincing results is to go granular, measuring the impact of specific initiatives and actions. In addition, innovation will impact cross-functional metrics, like brand value or employee experience and retention, so those should always be considered as well. Creating and tracking simple, useable metrics that make sense for you and your team is absolutely necessary. And make sure to always have them handy; innovation is one area where you have to constantly justify yourself—which, by the way, always works to your advantage.

## Incentivize Innovation through Radical Transparency

When we know what actions and results we're rewarded for, we tend to focus on them. The only way we know what these are, however, is through transparent goals and performance metrics. Therefore, instead of mandating, requiring, or forcing innovation, the best way to put this mindset and attitude into action is to incentivize the behavior that supports it. For example, if your compensation is directly connected to an activity metric like training a certain number of employees in an "innovation method" or an impact metric like revenue growth within a new customer segment, you're certainly going to take steps toward completing those goals. The completion of these metrics should help lead to growth and the company's well-being over the long term, not just short-term gains.

Imagine what it would be like if corporation and business leaders were compensated not on how well their business did today, but how well it did a year from today. We'd live in a very different world. Decisions would be made in an entirely new way, since thinking about the future would be as critical as thinking about the here and now. As discussed in the introduction, it's no secret that, regardless of the stated multiyear goals, the mentality of most organization's leaders is to maximize yield from whatever is right in front of them, rather than building a path toward the future. Such an attitude causes them to focus only on what's being delivered right now, as compared to the environment around them that will affect what happens later on. In fact, it would do wonders for your organization if you could directly tie promotions and compensation to executing on new ideas that led to sustainable growth. You would see a totally new behavior, benefitting everyone in the organization, and perhaps the world.

To truly incentivize innovation, and build a real culture of empowerment, your business metrics, and performance against them, must also be transparent—radically so. Whether looking at successes or failures, without understanding the metrics or seeing the actual results, employees—and leaders—will quickly disengage and lose focus, pretty much nullifying your entire investment in innovation. Or if they don't know what they're doing wrong, they'll never be able to fix the problem. So when you share results, make sure to publish them all—the good, the bad, the ugly—not just some sugar-coated selective messaging. You'll feel liberated, I promise.

In our culture, however, we're not always so forthcoming about the truth, the whole truth, and nothing but the truth. Corporations regularly show positive results and data to their employees, avoiding bad news, because they don't want to excite their workforce. PR departments do the same with consumers, focusing not on the whole picture, but just on the bright side. Company leaders who fudge the results aren't doing anyone, including themselves, any favors in the long run. They also risk losing their employees' trust and respect; if employees think their leaders are being dishonest or that the metrics do not reflect reality, then they'll stop paying attention to any of the metrics that are published. Executives themselves will give up on them as well.

I experienced this dismal reality at one of my first jobs. Among my duties, I was in charge of producing a robust metrics scorecard every week. I'd spend hours putting together an Excel spreadsheet detailing our company's marketing campaign execution against investment. Then I'd send it out by email to key executives in the department. Each time I sent the report, I'd receive responses like "Great job!" or "Fantastic!" or "So interesting!" But there was one problem: the metrics were actually showing that the project was in trouble and its performance was declining. So I tried a little experiment. One week, I password protected the Excel spreadsheet before sending it out. To my amusement, I received the same positive responses, but not one person asked me for the password—obviously, no one was reading the report. So, a few weeks later, I just stopped producing the report and invested my free time in surfing the web. And no: no one ever asked about those numbers again.

I don't blame the leadership for not reading the report; on the contrary, since I stopped producing it and no one noticed, they had indirectly given me the gift of free time. I also now understand where they were coming from—they were just so used to seeing massaged, BS metrics and results that they didn't expect anything different or actionable in these reports. It's also obvious that their compensation wasn't based on these metrics. If it was, I guarantee I would have been getting requests for that password in a second. Instead, no one paid attention and the metrics never really improved. I left soon after.

So it's not just transparency in metrics, which I was offering, but an understanding by everyone involved that these metrics matter. Even if the results are painful—and there will certainly be times when they are—clear metrics will create clear actions and results. If these results, and the decision-making processes that come from them, remain murky and are only transparent (or at least understandable) to a select few leaders, then the vast majority of a company won't know what they're being rewarded for, or not rewarded for. A transparent model, however, shows where resources are being invested, and why, and highlights the specific outcomes of these specific investments. Think about how many people working for you know what their team is really measured on and how they are performing against these benchmarks.

### Let's Be Honest

Transparency isn't always easy, in part because it requires a bluntness that can make some people rather uncomfortable. But when it comes to measuring success, we must be frank about bad ideas, especially if they come from our leaders. The general innovation management approach today is that there are "no bad ideas." But let's admit it—every day we all hear plenty of ideas that should not be implemented whatsoever. We of course need to provide time for ideas to develop and create safe spaces where we can all freely discuss concepts and opinions, giving us all the opportunity to listen to ideas, no matter how harebrained they may seem, and provide constructive feedback. Still, this doesn't mean all ideas are good ideas.

Some ideas might just be absolutely ridiculous, while others can be irrelevant, have limited benefits, or produce a low ROI. Then there are those that are actually very good, but they don't fit with organizational priorities or realities. If you truly want to create a real environment for innovation, your feedback must be clear, actionable, and honest. Yes, employees need a safe place to talk and generate ideas without judgment—probably even more so when it comes to large corporations—but once folks understand how ideas are measured, and why some of them are acted upon versus others, they come to a better conclusion of what works, what might work, and most importantly, what won't work.

Be honest up front: if employees suggest ideas that are not acted upon, they need to know why; as a leader you owe them that much and they deserve such respect. Because they're people too, of course, but it makes good business sense as well—they will create better results if they know how ideas are being measured, what's being celebrated and why, and what's better left on the cutting room floor. And if an idea is great, then don't wait around; *act on it and act on it fast*, otherwise you will discredit your entire efforts and demotivate your workforce.

Innovation happens in an environment when employees can openly provide their thoughts and input, and feel empowered to take action, and in which leadership is transparent about how and why they're moving forward with certain ideas and not others. This openness creates further learning opportunities for everyone involved. Transparent actions and clear metrics will incentivize your workforce, help them maintain focus, and lead to positive results. So metrics can be used not only to measure the effects of innovation but also to inspire innovation. They can also serve another crucial purpose, by alerting leadership, and employees, of when it's time to take a step back or go full speed ahead.

## Time It Right

When executing on your innovation strategy, results take time. In most cases, dramatic changes don't just occur, and new products and services don't just appear, overnight, even though it may feel like they do sometimes. (Does anyone remember Pokémon Go's global takeover?) Strategy must first be developed with employee input, socialized cross-functionally, funded, and executed; only then can it be measured. Whether you're looking at quarterly results or those for the fiscal year, innovation needs months to take hold, maybe even years depending on the desired outcome.

Consider the Nespresso coffee machine, the luxury at-home coffee and espresso maker that has taken the world by storm. The patent for the Nespresso system was filed in 1976, but the successful global rollout did not begin until 2000,[21] after which Nespresso became Nestle's fastest-growing product, up 40 percent annually.[22] That journey took some twists and turns, from Nespresso becoming a separate subsidiary of Nestle with five employees in 1986 to opening up the first Nespresso boutique in Paris in 2000,[23] to becoming the world's leading coffee company with 12,000 employees.[24]

Obviously, innovation needs time, but how much is too much or too little? Stakeholders need to know that change is taking place and your activity and strategy is consistently translating into a measurable impact. Of course, you don't want to go to market with a half-baked product or service, or get there too early with a near-perfect product or service only to find that no one is going to adopt it. For example, when I get online during flights, which I regularly do, I often think of Connexion by Boeing, a short-lived partnership between United Airlines, Delta Air Lines, American

Airlines, and Lufthansa. Connexion pioneered inflight Internet access and live-streaming TV, and was later widely picked up by other airlines, but there was little consumer adoption when it first came out in 2001.[25]

Within five years, Boeing decided to shut down Connexion, stating, "the market for the service has not materialized as had been expected."[26] Shortly thereafter, the iPhone was launched, generating unprecedented demand for Wi-Fi and creating an instant market for Wi-Fi coverage on planes. Today, I can't imagine flying without Wi-Fi, and given that I unfortunately almost always choose work over meditation, I easily shell out about $20 per flight to connect in the skies. Apparently I'm not alone: according to the third Inflight Connectivity Survey, published by the telecommunications company Inmarsat in 2018, 66 percent of passengers who think Wi-Fi is fundamental to daily life also believe that it is no longer a luxury in the air, and instead consider it an inflight necessity.[27] As we stay connected in the air, we contribute to a multibillion-dollar business that Boeing Connexion missed by only a year or so. In its 2017 report, the London School of Economics estimated that the airline connectivity market will be worth $130 billion in 2035, contributing $30 billion to airline revenue.[28]

Nespresso's timing was spot on, Boeing Connexion was too early, and there are of course plenty of companies that were too late and died young. Luck certainly plays a role, but the right metrics will always be your strongest indicator of whether or not "now" is the time, if you need to hold off, or, maybe worst of all, if you're spinning your wheels. It may be somewhat subjective, but if you're not seeing concrete results from your strategy in a reasonable amount of time that works for your business, then there's no point in going down the same innovation path; it's time to reconsider, shelve the project and maybe revisit it later, or pivot entirely. Whenever you start a new project, remind yourself that the future is unpredictable so innovation must be flexible. Such flexibility keeps teams open to the environment around them and the potential opportunities it presents. You should also expect the actual results to vary and remind yourself that unexpected outcomes can lead to major breakthroughs.

From Teflon to cornflakes, many new products were invented by accident. Port wine is just one more example. By the second half of the fifteenth century, the Portuguese and the British were regularly trading goods, especially Portuguese wine in exchange for English salt cod. Eventually, the vineyards along the Douro River were found to produce the preferred wine for the British connoisseurs, but to get the vino to England, it had to be shipped up the Atlantic—not a quick skip and a jump away in those days. The wine was therefore fortified with brandy, to protect it from spoiling. Today, the added brandy is essential to the taste of this sought-after "fortified" wine.[29]

Not all unintended outcomes are as rich and sweet as port, though, and many miss the mark entirely. We all have an illusion of control in our lives, but if we're honest with ourselves, that's about as far as it goes. Just as we as individuals do our best to create structure and order, so do organizations. The same holds true for innovation. We must admit when we're trying something new and that it must be measured, because first and foremost we're running a business and our strategy has an impact on others. If we consistently hit dead ends as we start execution, then it's probably time to reconsider our efforts, cut our losses, or go another route.

As the leader, you need to think about the best interests of your team and be the one to make the final decision on when to act, when to give in, and when to move on and try something new. Paying attention to data will give you the answer as to what to do next, so the metrics are all-important. If done with attention, care, and skill, consistent, transparent measurement of innovation's impact will create insight into what's working—and what's not—and provide the overall organization with an opportunity to improve and continue innovating.

## Case Study: TripAdvisor

International travel is booming. With the world being so open and connected, the growth of spending on international tourism has outpaced that of global GDP.[30] In 2017, tourism spending was $5.29 trillion, and one company alone was responsible for influencing 10.3 percent, or $546 billion, of it: TripAdvisor.[31] Founded in 2000, TripAdvisor has quickly become the go-to place for hotel reviews and bookings, as well as other travel-related information or content, with 456 million people visiting the site every month to plan a trip (just for a little perspective, that's one in every sixteen people on earth).[32] TripAdvisor has expanded into the TripAdvisor Media Group, operating 25 travel brands all over the world.

Stephen Kaufer came up with the TripAdvisor idea somewhat by accident, without any intention of launching such a massive venture. While trying to plan a trip to Mexico with his wife, Caroline, Kaufer became frustrated over the lack of unbiased opinions on numerous websites he kept reading about a particular hotel, all of which featured the same photos and advertising copy. He finally tracked down what he considered an unbiased review, which came from two people who'd actually stayed at the hotel in question, and it turned out the place was not up to par as advertised.

Caroline suggested to her husband that he create a simple website, "easy to use and honest" that would help travelers who find themselves in the same situation.[33] Kaufer thought it over, and shortly after launched the site, relying on the same type of simple, crowdsourced, user-generated content that companies like Yelp use. These real reviews by real people have led to solving customer problems, creating an actual community around user engagement, and ultimately generating profits, all of which rely on metrics. These factors have built TripAdvisor into a multibillion-dollar company.[34]

TripAdvisor's customers consist of community members who write reviews about their travel experiences, advertisers, and people who read the reviews but do not contribute to the site. The metrics are easy to gauge here: community members provide star ratings and reviews based on their personal experiences,

*(continued)*

## Case Study: TripAdvisor (*continued*)

sharing the knowledge they've gained in visiting the places in question. The second group, advertisers, measure their success on the conversion rate between TripAdvisor and hotel bookings. The third group, those who read the reviews but do not contribute, spend their money and time based on what they've read on the site, believing in the reviews' quality and honesty. You cannot sell anything to any of these audiences without metrics and transparency.

You may be thinking, that's how all crowdsourced reviews work; what's so different about TripAdvisor? Well it's not just the service that relies on the metrics, but what lies behind the curtain as well. Kaufer is well known for two signs that he has placed on the door of his office: "Speed wins" and "If it's worth doing, it's worth measuring."[35] He certainly knows a thing or two about timing, and he also believes that CEOs must understand what a proposal's success looks like, and how it will "matter in a big way for the company."[36] As further reported by *Innovation Leader*, "Establishing a metric or two, Kaufer explained, was essential to understanding if the idea was resonating with customers and living up to its potential—or if it merely sounded sexy in the confines of a conference room."[37]

In this way, metrics have been essential to both the company's internal and external success. Kaufer understood the dilemma at hand, developed a clear strategy to solve the problem, and found a way to measure the results every step of the way. His "speed wins" approach also means that reviews can be accessed quickly, anytime and anywhere with a Wi-Fi signal. Based on speed and metrics, Kaufer didn't just create the largest social travel website in the world or a new market—he's helped create a whole new way to travel.

## Summary: Metrics Matter

Innovation is all about concrete results, and results must be measured. If your strategy doesn't move the needle, then you're not innovating. Activity and impact metrics must be considered, and much of the impact eventually comes down to dollars and cents—you need to be able to quantify innovation in order to continue championing it. If you don't, you'll never be able to prove that the mindset and attitude that's enabling these outcomes even exists, and you certainly won't be able to use metrics to further drive results. Clearly showing the effectiveness and impact of innovation is at the center of creating a culture of innovation, and without incentives to innovate, you're going to have trouble getting anyone on board. And without results your culture remains just a culture.

Innovation behaviors should be incentivized through metrics. Leadership must be transparent about how and why they're investing in one initiative over the other because this openness creates learning opportunities and helps people understand what works and what doesn't. The actual results measured might not match the intended ones and staying flexible and communicating clearly can help turn these unexpected outcomes into a positive, or bring to light another area in which to innovate. Still, you need to know when to pack it in and move on. Doing so isn't always easy, and it's possible that you'll start second-guessing every move you make. The best way to get over this hump is to get back to the basics. Not every innovation strategy needs to have a dramatic, disruptive, life-changing goal in mind, and as we'll explore in the next chapter, it's better to start with easy-to-measure, small milestones.

### Principle

Innovation must be measured. Metrics help innovation take root and grow throughout the organization.

### Action

- Find the balanced measurements that are right for your organization and industry, giving attention to both activity and impact metrics.
- Get stakeholders and leadership to buy in to these metrics.
- Measure and transparently communicate performance.
- Give innovation time to develop and know when to pivot or take the project to the next level.

(*continued*)

*(continued)*

### Obstacle

Expectations are often misaligned throughout an organization and there is an imbalance between activity and impact. Leaders sometimes sugarcoat the data and publish selective metrics that show only positive results, or don't even follow metrics at all.

### Outcome

Clear, measurable goals and metrics that drive the decision-making process, with focused efforts and transparency that enables innovation by providing individuals and teams opportunities to improve.

## Notes

1. Case Western Reserve University, "Mindfulness in the workplace improves employee focus, attention, behavior, new management-based research concludes," *Science Daily: Science News*, March 10, 2016, https://www.sciencedaily.com/releases/2016/03/160310141455.htm.
2. David Gelles, "At Aetna, a C.E.O.'s Management by Mantra," *New York Times*, February 27, 2015, https://www.nytimes.com/2015/03/01/business/at-aetna-a-ceos-management-by-mantra.html.
3. Ibid.
4. Case Western Reserve University, "Mindfulness."
5. Gelles, "At Aetna."
6. Todd Spangler, "Are Americans Addicted to Smartphones? U.S. Consumers Check Their Phones 52 Times Daily Study Finds," *Variety*, November 14, 2018, https://variety.com/2018/digital/news/smartphone-addiction-study-check-phones-52-times-daily-1203028454/.

7. Esther Perel, Twitter post, June 18, 2018, https://twitter.com/EstherPerel/status/1008877076634619908.
8. Bethany Mclean and Peter Elkind, "The Guiltiest Guys in the Room," *CNN Money*, July 5, 2006, https://money.cnn.com/2006/05/29/news/enron_guiltyest/.
9. Jeff Shore, "These 10 Peter Drucker Quotes May Change Your World," *Entrepreneur*, September 16, 2014, https://www.entrepreneur.com/slideshow/299936.
10. Hilary Potkewitz, "Headspace vs. Calm: The Meditation Battle That's Anything but Zen," *Wall Street Journal*, December 15, 2018, https://www.wsj.com/articles/headspace-vs-calm-the-meditation-battle-thats-anything-but-zen-11544889606.
11. Andy Puddicombe, "About Headspace," Headspace.com, 2019, https://www.headspace.com/about-us.
12. Iris Kuo, "Headspace's Ultimate Guide to Employee Productivity," *Gusto*, February 28, 2018, https://gusto.com/blog/growth/headspace-productivity.
13. Craft, "Headspace," Craft.co, 2019, https://craft.co/headspace.
14. Steph Solis, "Ringling Bros. Circus Closing after 146 Years," *USA Today,* January 14, 2017, https://www.usatoday.com/story/news/nation/2017/01/14/ringling-bros-circus-close-after-146-years/96606820/.
15. Mark Rendell, "Cirque du Soleil Acquires Blue Man Group Production Company," *Globe and Mail*, July 6, 2017, https://www.theglobeandmail.com/report-on-business/cirque-du-soleil-acquires-blue-man-group-production-company/article35574125/.
16. Innovation Leader, *Untangling Innovation Metrics*, Innovation Leader Research, Spring 2015, https://www.innovationleader.com/2015-metrics-report/.

17. Ibid.
18. Ibid.
19. Ibid.
20. Ibid.
21. Rob Sharp, "The Cult of Nespresso," *Independent*, October 4, 20017, https://www.independent.co.uk/life-style/food-and-drink/features/the-cult-of-nespresso-could-it-really-be-the-best-cup-of-coffee-money-can-buy-395944.html.
22. RPARK, "Brewing a Successful Future at Nespresso?" *Harvard Business School*, April 30, 2018.
23. Nestlé Nespresso SA, "The Nespresso History: From a Simple Idea to a Unique Brand Experience," Corporate Communications, May 2016, https://www.nestle-nespresso.com/asset-library/documents/nespresso%20-%20history%20factsheet.pdf.
24. Nestlé Nespresso SA, "Corporate Background," Corporate Communications, May 2016, https://www.nestle-nespresso.com/asset-library/documents/nespresso%20-%20corporate%20backgrounder.pdf.
25. Boeing, "American, Delta and United Airlines Join with Connexion by Boeing to Pursue Broadband Inflight Connectivity Venture," Boeing: Media, June 13, 2001, https://web.archive.org/web/20100605041051/http://www.boeing.com/news/releases/2001/q2/news_release_010613a.html.
26. John Dern, "Boeing to Discontinue Connexion by Boeing Service," Boeing News Release, August 17, 2006, https://web.archive.org/web/20060820174419/http:/www.boeing.com/news/releases/2006/q3/060817a_nr.html.
27. Inmarsat, "Inflight Connectivity Survey," Inmarsat, 2018, https://www.inmarsat.com/aviation/commercial-aviation/in-flight-connectivity-survey/.

28. Alexander Grous, "Sky High Economics," LSE Consulting, September 2017, http://www.lse.ac.uk/business-and-consultancy/consulting/consulting-reports/sky-high-economics.

29. Tatiana Livesy, "A 3 Minute History of Port Wine," *Winerist*, December 4, 2015, https://www.winerist.com/magazine/wine/a-3-minute-history-of-port-wine.

30. TripAdvisor Strategic Insights and Oxford Economics, "Sizing Worldwide Tourism Spending (or "GTP") & TripAdvisor's Economic Impact," TripAdvisor Strategic Insights and Oxford Economics, 2017, https://mk0tainsights9mcv7wv.kinstacdn.com/wp-content/uploads/2018/09/Worldwide-Tourism-Economics-2017-compressed.pdf.

31. Ibid.

32. Linda Kinstler, "How TripAdvisor Changed Travel," *Guardian*, August 17, 2018, https://www.theguardian.com/news/2018/aug/17/how-tripadvisor-changed-travel.

33. Stephen Kaufer, "An Average Traveler," *New York Times*, February 23, 2013, https://www.nytimes.com/2013/02/24/jobs/stephen-kaufer-of-tripadvisor-is-an-average-traveler.html.

34. Kinstler, "How TripAdvisor Changed Travel."

35. Innovation Leader, *Untangling Innovation Metrics*.

36. Ibid.

37. Ibid.

# Chapter 4

## Innovation Is *Not* Disruption

There's only one word that may be buzzier than "innovation," one that universally strikes fear into the heart of established companies across industries while also being used as the battle cry for the hottest startups in the Valley: *disruption.* It's all about disruption these days, isn't it? At least that's what everyone would have you believe. Proof of disruption of one kind or another surrounds us; look at healthcare, entertainment, science and technology, news, education, engineering, the environment, social media—nearly everything. But just because disruption's taking place doesn't mean that every innovation, system, or idea needs to be "disruptive" in response.

Take duty-free shopping, for example. Anyone who has ever traveled internationally by plane is familiar with the concept. When passengers get through security and head to their gates, they often must go through the mazelike obstacle of duty-free shops, offering a range of products from booze to cologne, makeup to candy. The experience reminds me of staying in a hotel in Las Vegas, with the mandatory walk through on the casino floor, the flashing games pleading to be played, as you head from the entrance in the lobby to the elevators to your room. Duty-free products are exempt from specific national or local taxes and duties, as long as the buyers will be taking them out of the country. If you sit and watch the number of people going in and out of one of these shops, you probably won't be surprised to hear that in 2017, global duty-free sales, combined with other travel retail sales, added up to around $68.6 billion.[1]

The simple idea of offering tax-exempt products at airports got its start in Shannon, Ireland, in 1950, when an enterprising bartender, caterer, and hotel clerk named Brendan O'Regan discovered a loophole in British Isles law. There had been a tradition that went back *hundreds* of years in which sailors could purchase alcohol without paying duties before they shipped out to sea. Though the international cruise ships had caught on and were able to serve cheap booze as they puttered across the ocean, the same idea had not been applied anywhere else.

At the time, O'Regan was working at the Shannon airport, handling food and drink services, and catering mostly to wealthy Americans. In those days, transatlantic commercial flights from the US to Europe had to make a pit stop in Shannon to refuel, consistently bringing more and more passengers to the airport. O'Regan saw cruise ships as direct competitors for these international flights, and therefore as his rivals. It seemed unfair that they had a leg up with inexpensive beer and liquor, so he lobbied the government for duty-free alcohol and tobacco in airports, claiming that not only would it be good for business, but it would attract more tourist dollars to the country. And he was right.

The success of the duty-free model caught on elsewhere quickly. Amsterdam opened the second duty-free location in 1957, and in 1962, the US's first duty-free shop was established in Hawaii.[2] Of course, O'Regan didn't come up with the tax-free products, and he based his concept on the cruise ship model after he had been a passenger on one from the US back home to Ireland. Still, it certainly panned out: Global duty-free sales, combined with other travel retail sales, is expected to hit $125.1 billion by 2023.[3] In 2016, South Korea's Incheon Airport made $2 billion in duty-free sales alone, crowning it the king of duty-free as the largest duty-free airport market in the world, by sales, beating out Dubai Duty Free, which sold "only" $1.85 billion of duty-free products that year.[4]

Duty-free probably isn't the first thing you think when you hear "innovation," but maybe it should be. O'Regan worked with his key stakeholders, the airport and the government, to gain their support, and he capitalized on the captive travelers who had plenty of free time at the terminals, making their stay much better, while also parting them from their money. The shopping was pleasurable and resulted in a variety of products and savings. The model was then picked up and iterated throughout the globe. It was a practical innovation—nothing "disruptive" at face value—that was hugely successful and made a lasting mark on international travel.

Today, whenever the concept of innovation comes up, the word "disruption" is likely to creep in behind it. In fact, it's mentioned so much in relation to innovation that many people think innovation *is* disruption, and vice versa. But innovation and disruption are *not* the same—don't get them confused. Disruption can be seen as a rapid evolution in business or technology, perhaps one that comes unexpectedly for many and has a significant impact; but it's also just another word for change. As discussed, change can't be stopped, and if we want our organizations and communities to survive and thrive, it must be met with innovation and embraced. Innovation can, of course, lead to disruption, but it doesn't have to, nor should it always. Before you try creating the next "big thing," first focus on your strategy and the related metrics that you'd like to move. Innovation doesn't need to be complicated or complex—sometimes the simplest, most elegant solution is the best.

## Stop Thinking "Disruptively"

Thinking "disruptively" is counterproductive nonsense, and not applicable in most settings. There seems to be a popular opinion that disruption is always a good thing and always necessary, but neither notion is true. First, disruption must be considered in relation to the context in which you operate; what may seem disruptive to one company or industry may not be as critical to another.

Second, relying on "disruption" as a strategy or plan immediately creates a mindset based on the assumption that what every company needs, and what every team member needs to produce, is that magical billion-dollar idea that alters the foundation of everything we know about a business, concept, or approach—a cataclysmic burst of creativity that rocks the world. The fact remains, however, that these events are rare. Instead, when disruptive changes occur, they are usually the result of a long chain of events. Call it the snowball effect, the tipping point, or critical mass; something cracks in numerous places before it's broken wide open.

This combination of earlier events and circumstances creates disruption. Think about e-books, for example. Though they seem to be totally disruptive to print, and therefore the entire publishing industry, they are actually a part of a long tradition that goes back to Gutenberg in the 1400s, or even six hundred years earlier when, as some scholars argue, the first printed books appeared.[5] Then again, e-book sales from traditional publishers have been hovering around 20–25 percent of the total book market for a number of years—not quite the disruptive change they were cracked up to be.[6]

Audiobooks, however, may prove to be an actual disruptor. In 2017, sales of audiobooks increased by about 20 percent, year over year, across the publishing industry.[7] During that same time, print was up 1.5 percent and e-book sales actually fell by 5.4 percent.[8] An increase in demand for the auditory literary experience has been brought on by the widespread adoption of voice assistants, use of smartphones, new apps from companies like Scribd, and an increase in services and companies focused on audiobooks alone, such as Amazon's Audible. With so many titles out there, though, the only way to convert them all to audio is to involve artificial intelligence.

If you've ever read—ahem—*listened* to one of these books featuring a friendly artificial intelligence voice, it's easy to recognize a lack of intonation and empathy. Once that issue gets fully solved, though, the sales numbers are likely to go through the roof. Still, that will just be another step in the long history of books—we certainly didn't jump from the invention of moveable type to listening to audiobooks in our electric cars in a blink of an eye.

Though audiobooks may not yet be considered a disruption to the publishing, education, or entertainment industries, streaming music has been entirely, and truly, disruptive to the recording industry. But again, it's another link in a long chain, not just a lightning-bolt event. Look at the evolution of recorded music; just as with books, it's a history of technological advances. Without the analog LP, we wouldn't have had the analog tape (or the godforsaken eight-track tape) or the digital CD. Without the CD we wouldn't have had MP3s. Without these files, we wouldn't have had Napster, nor would we have ended up streaming an infinite library of music in a moment's notice via Spotify and YouTube. Yes, the recording industry has changed—okay, "been disrupted"—but that didn't happen overnight.

As a leader, if you try to "orchestrate disruption," you're going to fall flat on your face. Instead, you need to focus on a clear vision, pragmatic strategy, and execution in small measurable milestones. Avoid putting all your eggs in the "disruption" basket; find a way to build on what exists, keeping in mind that innovation is most often a sequential process. If you encourage everyone to start "innovating disruptively" you're likely setting them up for failure. You're also dividing your employees into two classes—those who believe they can come up with that "billion-dollar idea" and those who believe they can't (and of course, most can't or won't).

"Disruptive innovation," "billion-dollar ideas," the creation of "second-class" employees: it all adds up to one big mind game, and not a useful one. If, instead, everyone is on the same team, working to put an innovative strategy into action, innovation is more likely to grow. (By the way, those members of the team who do by chance come up with a billion-dollar, disruptive idea—and those are indeed rare—are more likely to take the concept and go elsewhere, keeping the fortune and accolades for themselves.) The aim should be to create value by solving a problem. So rather than thinking and innovating disruptively, think *about* disruption, and understand how innovation can help create opportunities from the changes taking place around you.

### Turn Disruption into an Opportunity

Though we often think about Spotify, Amazon, Google, Netflix, Facebook, and other new tech giants as disrupting specific industries, businesses across all sorts of sectors are feeling the disruption blues. According to a 2018 report by Accenture, in which the firm surveyed 3,600 companies with at least $100 million in annual revenues from across 82 countries, 63 percent stated that they were facing high levels of disruption, while 44 percent believed there were severe signs showing their susceptibility to disruption in the future.[9]

It sounds scary, but this situation also presents opportunities that would have otherwise been unavailable in the past. In the short run, innovation is the only way to respond *to* disruption, but in the long run, innovation is the only way to evolve *with* it. Just as innovation requires foresight, you need to look at potentially disruptive threats and consider them seriously. Again, keep in mind that I'm talking about change here: it continues to come even when you don't want it to and you can't let it hit you unprepared.

For example, many public utilities were not prepared for solar power, but its sudden growth has resulted in lost revenue, forcing utilities to rethink the whole system. Even in 2016, a survey of 150 senior energy industry executives was released that stated that almost 70 percent of respondents cited the growth in renewable technologies as "the most disruptive trend shaping"[10] the energy sector. As Jonathan Weisgall, vice president of government relations at Berkshire Hathaway Energy reported at the time, "Our monopoly days are coming to an end. We are in a competitive market, and we have to recognize that as a utility."[11]

It's somewhat ironic, and a bit funny, that if energy companies were to look back at their industry, they would note that it has always been completely made up of continuous change, another chain of events to get us to where we are today. From wood and coal to gas to nuclear to solar and wind, these advancements have regularly disrupted how we power our homes, businesses, and vehicles. It's amazing that executives of these companies seem to be caught off guard every single time a new source emerges, even when the writing is on the wall.

There was a time when monopolies didn't worry much about customers, and they weren't all that concerned with disruption. Regulations kept many companies afloat, and if you were a monopoly, you likely had the mindset "Well, where else are our customers going to go? Nowhere!" Now that every industry is more competitive, with greater choice for consumers, companies need to offer more customer value. Otherwise they'll keep losing business. Energy executives have therefore started paying attention and begun diversifying their portfolio, investing in solar and other renewable sources of energy.

And though renewable energy and traditional utilities are often pitted against one another, it's not necessarily that the companies refuse to change. It's true that in some states, legislation has been put in place to diminish solar—to great outcry—but many utilities claim it's more a question of logistics. As Tanuj Deora, the executive president at the Smart Electric Power Alliance, said in a 2017 interview, the slow adaptation was "not because they have some hatred for rooftop solar," but because reworking all of their systems for renewable energy was incredibly difficult and involved.[12] The networks simply weren't prepared for such major change. In time, it's likely that the adjustments will be made—they must be.

Then there are ridesharing companies like Uber and Lyft. You probably think I'm about to explain how they're putting taxis out of business. Though that's true, their effects are much wider-ranging, as seen with the declining revenue of airports. Now that a ride to and from the airport is just a click away on their smart phones, flyers are opting out of leaving their cars in long-term parking, hailing taxis or calling them the night before a big trip, or renting cars at their final destination.[13] Before 2012, when ridesharing apps took off, private cars, taxis, and rental cars made up 80–90 percent of roundtrips to airports (the rest were handled by dedicated rail lines).[14] As of 2017, ridesharing apps accounted for 62 percent of business traveler expenditure (up from 8 percent just three years earlier, in 2014).[15]

Though you may not have guessed it by the price of your ticket, airports depend on the money you spend on car rentals, parking lots, and taxis—those are the biggest sources of revenue aside from the fees the airlines pay to use the airports. Parking alone makes up a quarter of airports' total operating revenue.[16] In 2016, when adding in rentals and taxis, it all totaled up to 42 percent of the $9.6 billion airports collected in fees that year.[17] Airports were paid an additional $1.8 billion by rental car companies.[18] Between that 42 percent and $1.8 billion, they were looking at around $5.8 billion that year—far more than the fees they get from restaurants, stores, and hotels.[19]

As ridesharing has become convenient, affordable, and widely adopted, one of airports' core revenue streams has begun to disappear. In response, airports are starting to work with this disruption, not against it. From Changi Airport in Singapore, to Paris–Charles de Gaulle in France, to San Diego, airports are launching "innovation labs." These programs pull together some of the best minds from different areas dedicated to finding solutions to the problems that airports are facing, looking for ways to create new value for their customers as they wait for their flights, just like Brendan O'Regan did with his duty-free shopping. This unexpected disruption is forcing airports to innovate with a clear purpose and a focus on improving metrics such as revenue, customer satisfaction, and operational efficiency. As they try to find new opportunities, instead of searching for a pie-in-the-sky disruptive approach of their own, they should move forward in the same way as all the other companies experiencing the effects of disruption should—clearly and pragmatically.

## Start Thinking Pragmatically

I fully admit that "pragmatic innovation" isn't the sexiest term, but it best describes the process that is central to innovation: creating a bold vision and strategy, setting reasonable goals, and executing that vision and strategy in small, measurable milestones. You can dress it up and call it whatever you want to inspire your team, but make sure to stick to the message: pragmatic innovation is all that counts. Many leaders are fond of statements like "shoot for the moon," but unless you are in the business of space exploration, this is totally useless. Don't start big; start small. Measurable execution over time creates experience, credibility, and true innovation.

But a focus on disruption, not innovation, persists. I remember speaking to a colleague of mine about a consulting gig he once had. A company called him in to help their team in charge of developing new products and services get over a seemingly perpetual slump. The first day he walked into the conference room to meet the team members, a poster on the wall caught his eye. Printed in large letters and numbers was "FY10: Getting Closer to Capturing a Billion-Dollar Idea." What really grabbed his attention though, is that the "FY10," for "fiscal year ten," had a number of Post-it Notes all over it. He walked up to inspect and realized that each one had another fiscal year written on it, "FY11," "FY12," "FY13." Obviously fiscal year ten had come and gone and the team wasn't much closer, if at all, to capturing and implementing that billion-dollar payday idea.

Pragmatically speaking, the team needed to create a concrete, attainable target and refocus their energy toward executing in small measurable milestones. Instead, they were stuck thinking that the only way to be really innovative (or maybe be promoted) was through some type of strategic, major disruption—as if you could strategize disruption from an executive boardroom. When you complete small, measurable steps, you gain experience and build credibility and trust with your stakeholders, not to mention a stronger self-esteem. In the process, leaders and employees then develop an appetite for further innovation, leading to greater growth and success.

Pragmatic innovation requires gradual, steady progress, each step building on the previous one. It may seem counterintuitive, but this step-by-step process will get your product or service to market faster in the end, and with much better odds of success. Instead of wracking your brain for billion-dollar ideas, you'll be producing results that make sense for your business. Remember, innovation is all about execution, not disruption. And contrary to popular belief, executing on innovation strategy doesn't always need to be complicated; in many ways it's no different than any other project.

## Get Back to the Basics

Disruption in the twenty-first century is directly related to the technological advances we're experiencing in the Fourth Industrial Revolution. And since people tend to confuse disruption with innovation, everyone assumes that to make an impact, all innovation must be extremely high-tech too. That's one of the reasons many leaders are so anxious when it comes to technology, thinking about artificial intelligence, augmented reality, autonomous transportation, blockchain, cloud computing, deep learning, drones, edge computing, genomics, the Internet of Things, machine learning, robotics, self-driving (and even self-flying) cars, quantum computing, voice assistants, voice recognition, virtual reality, 3D printing, 5G—you name it. I call this line of thought "techno-FOMO." We're so scared of missing out on the latest, greatest tech, we forget that what we should really be focusing on is value. When evaluating new technology, we need to look at it in practical terms, considering its utility and application, and what it can make possible or enable. We absolutely need to know about the emerging technology advances as part of our environment, but we don't need to act on every single one. Tech is not what solves problems—innovators do.

If we start with the basics, not the tech, then we will have a clearer vision of what we're trying to accomplish and why. Would-be innovators need to get over tech as a religion and innovate with a pragmatic purpose. Of course, technology is important, but we must start with the customer problem we want to solve or the value we want to create for ourselves or others, then figure out how to get there. That's why we're all here: companies make money by solving problems or by generating new value. Sometimes technology plays a role in meeting human needs and demands, and sometimes it doesn't.

No matter how tech-heavy you are, innovation always improves on ideas of the past, making them relevant and useful today and into the future. At any given time, the most successful concepts have existed for years prior in one form or another. Take Instacart, a company that brings groceries right to your front door, or Postmates, which drops off more than groceries—including alcohol, prepared meals, and pretty much anything from any retail store—and features the slogan "Anything, anytime, anywhere. We get it."[20] Both companies are generating a lot of money. As of 2017, Instacart had more than 500,000 customers and an estimated $2 billion in revenue.[21] The company enables sales through the largest online grocery catalog, offering over half a billion items, with 300-plus retail partners across North America, 800 employees, and more than 70,000 shoppers.[22] Postmates, in the meantime, was valued at $1.85 billion in 2019 before its planned IPO.[23]

We're talking a lot of money. But let's face it: it's just delivery! It's basically no different than when you used to ring up the closest Chinese restaurant and order fried rice. Postmates and Instacart took an old idea, repackaged it at the right time, and found a way to meet new customer demands that ask, "Well if I can order takeout, why can't I order anything I want?" With the growing popularity of online retail and our love for instant gratification, it was only a matter of time for these new delivery services to take hold.

In fact, even before Postmates and Instacart, there was Webvan, the first web retailer to deliver groceries, founded way back in 1999.[24] Despite the fact that none of Webvan's senior executives had any experience in the supermarket industry, the company was able to attract nearly $400 million in venture funding,[25] followed by another $375 million through an IPO.[26] Even though the cumulative revenue of the company was only $395,000, and the cumulative losses were $50 million, Webvan was still valued at $7.9 billion when it went to market.[27] In the end, the company didn't pan out, shutting down in June 2001, after having lost over $800 million and firing 2,000 workers.[28] CNET called the company "one of the most epic fails in the dotcom bubble fiasco."[29]

Postmates, Instacart, and others took the Webvan model—really the food delivery model—and leveraged go-to market models of the day: the almighty app and the on-demand gig economy. Webvan spent most of their money buying trucks and warehouses to fill orders with their own teams, whereas these new companies own few assets, barely have employees, and developed a platform. The idea was basic, but new market realities and digital capabilities brought this delivery industry to life. It was really a matter of timing (a concept explored in Chapter 3). So here we see a melding of a low-tech (or no-tech) idea, with a high-tech component. In fact, most ideas are low-tech when it comes down to it, but they can be enabled by tech to create results. For example, the concept of space travel didn't start with the Apollo program; people have been thinking about traveling to the stars since humans first began paying attention to the night's sky.

Today, many of us can't imagine living without home delivery of all sorts of things, from consumer goods to meal kits. The market for grocery delivery also continues to grow and is expected to reach $100 billion by 2025, comprising 20 percent of grocery retail.[30] And who knows what's going to happen next? We might have 3D printers in one door of our fridge producing groceries on demand to put into the other door. You never can tell.

It's not what's "new," but what's *best* given the present, past, and foreseeable environment. People commonly ask me what innovation management software I use for "innovating." I always feel for these future innovators-to-be because it's obvious that they're passionate about driving change, but they get stuck focusing on the wrong priorities. As an initial step, they need to work on figuring out what goals they are trying to achieve with innovation, before worrying about what kind of software they're going to use. Otherwise, it's like they're starting a company by first designing a business card rather than figuring out the value they are going to provide to their potential customers. So, along with the other advice I give them, I always make sure to tell them to start at the beginning: take out a pen or pencil, grab a pad of paper, and brainstorm how to solve the problem at hand.

## Case Study: Dyson

Dyson products are known for a number of things: high quality, high price tag, and designs unlike any other. Before Dyson, few people would have ever thought of buying a $400 hair dryer or shelling out $500 for a fan with no blades and a huge hole in its center. But here we are. And how we got here is the story of an innovator who understood the need to improve on old products, iterate over time, and complete those small measurable milestones that are the foundation of true innovation.

In 1978, James Dyson came up with the concept of an "industrial cyclone tower" that used centrifugal force to remove dust and other particles from the air.[31] The young inventor soon realized he could use the filter technology in a vacuum, sucking up dirt and other debris into a cone-like structure that would then be forced out to the edges of the canister, with no bag required. This idea came from a practical issue he was having while redoing his home; otherwise it might never have occurred to him. After creating a cardboard prototype, which he built on top of his Hoover vacuum, he started to think that the industrial cyclone concept could have greater potential. So he pitched it to a number of possible investors in the vacuum marketplace, looking to see if anyone would be interested in licensing his idea, but every company he spoke to turned him down. They essentially told him, "That's just not how we do things here." I'd love to hear what they have to say now.

The experience didn't deter Dyson, and might even have inspired him. Over the next fifteen years, he developed 5,127

*(continued)*

## Case Study: Dyson (*continued*)

prototypes before landing on the vacuum cleaner that has since become synonymous with quality, not to mention design, and made him a household name.[32] Other innovators might have given up or settled for less, but not Dyson. His success is not in the technology or concept of the vacuum (the patent for the "pneumatic carpet renovator" was filed by J. S. Thurman in 1899[33]) but in his willingness to follow a process of small incremental changes—hundreds of them—that added up over time. As of 2019, Dyson is one of the UK's wealthiest individuals, worth an estimated $13.8 billion,[34] but he has something that many people consider even greater than that, an achievement that cannot be measured in money: a knighthood. In 2006, he became Sir James Dyson, knighted in the New Year's Honours List for "services to business."[35]

Though the Dyson company has expanded and diversified, it all started with the vacuum. Dyson took a practical approach; with no plans to disrupt the market, he was simply looking to make a better product, building an updated version and innovating on top of it repeatedly. Dyson's work was, and continues to be, pragmatic. He is passionate about metrics too: Dyson's engineers ensure quality control through stats, mathematical formulas, and sample testing at every stage.[36] When he realized that a washing machine they developed wasn't performing as well as he had hoped in the market, he cut his losses, learned from failure, and moved on. Later, the company extended its product portfolio by creating more iconic products such as its fans and hair dryers.

Dyson has a clear mission to design "iconic reinventions that work, perform and look very different."[37] You won't see "disruption" in this statement, though you will note "reinventions" is prominent, and in fact Sir James's motto is "Everything can improve."[38] He's always considering classic products that he can innovate upon and make better, whether that's a vacuum, a hair dryer, a fan, or a car. And of course, Dyson did end up disrupting the market eventually, practically killing the vacuum bag industry, but he only got there by starting with the basics. It's not "big tech" or even a "big idea," but an ability to think pragmatically and solve a problem step by step. If we put our minds to it, these are two things that any of us can do.

## Summary: The Pen Is Mightier than the Program

If we confuse "disruption" with "innovation," we miss the point. Innovation can lead to disruption and it can mitigate its effects, but the two are not one and the same. We need to be ready for disruptions, understanding the forces behind them and their aftereffects, but we also need to concentrate our efforts toward executing our strategy and moving our metrics toward our goals. If we constantly search for a disruption or a billion-dollar idea, we'll lose out on the steady growth and market adjacencies that come from observing our environment, developing comprehensive strategy, setting real goals, and executing actionable, measurable milestones. When we focus on pragmatic innovation, not disruption, we see real results add up.

Disruption, like innovation, should be seen as cumulative and constant, and there is no one-size-fits-all solution to dealing with its effects. To respond to and work with change, either big or small, focus on executing the best ideas, not the ones that have the fanciest names or the newest tech. Technology's great, but high-tech solutions aren't the answers to all our problems, even if so many of us believe they are. As much as you look into the future, also look to the past for inspiration, to understand what's happening around you, and to develop strategy that gets you closer to your goals. This grounded approach might not be as glamorous as chasing elusive billion-dollar ideas, and it's actually harder to implement since it's a massive undertaking that forces accountability. But if that sounds overwhelming, don't freak out quite yet: as discussed in the next chapter, you're not alone, and with the right team in place, innovation will flourish.

### Principle

Be pragmatic; not all innovations need to be "disruptive."

### Action

- Instead of "thinking disruptively" think pragmatically.
- Work with disruption to find new opportunities to create value and solve problems.

- Execute on strategy in small measurable milestones.
- Build on past successes and failures through a steady, incremental approach.

### Obstacle

Leaders are on the hunt for billion-dollar ideas, so the concept of moonshots takes precedence over small, measurable milestones. In the process, teams often lose touch with reality, focus on the high-tech flavor of the month, miss out on opportunities to innovate, and, in the end, fail.

### Outcome

A culture that understands and recognizes disruption, while focusing on a balanced strategy through reasonable goals and execution in small, measurable milestones.

## Notes

1. Statista, "Duty Free and Travel Retail Sales Worldwide from 2016 to 2023 (in Billion U.S. Dollars)," Statista.com, 2019, https://www.statista.com/statistics/478552/duty-free-travel-retail-sales-worldwide-forecast/.
2. Robert Smith and Jesse Barker, "#841: The Land of Duty Free," *National Public Radio*, May 11, 2018, https://www.npr.org/templates/transcript/transcript.php?storyId=610518433.
3. Statista, "Duty Free."
4. Charlotte Turner, "Incheon Airport Duty Free Sales Hit US$2bn in 2016," *TRBusiness*, January 16, 2017, https://www.trbusiness.com/regional-news/asia-pacific/incheon-airport-duty-free-sales-hit-us2bn-in-2016/114119.
5. Annalee Newitz, "Printed books existed nearly 600 years before Gutenberg's Bible," *Gizmodo*, May 14, 2012, https://io9.gizmodo.com/printed-books-existed-nearly-600-years-before-gutenberg-5910249.

6. Joshua Fruhlinger, "Are E-Books Finally Over? The Publishing Industry Unexpectedly Tilts Back to Print," *Observer*, November 3, 2018, https://observer.com/2018/11/ebook-sales-decline-independent-bookstores/.
7. Adam Rowe, "The Rising Popularity of Audiobooks Highlights the Industry's Backwards Pay Scale," *Forbes*, March 27, 2018, https://www.forbes.com/sites/adamrowe1/2018/03/27/the-rising-popularity-of-audiobooks-highlights-the-industrys-backwards-payscale/.
8. Ibid.
9. Alison DeNisco Rayome, "How companies can predict new tech disruption and fight back against it," *TechRepublic*, February 25, 2018, https://www.techrepublic.com/article/how-companies-can-predict-new-tech-disruption-and-fight-back-against-it/.
10. "Volatility, Disruption Driving Growth Strategies, M&A, Transformation In Energy Sector: KPMG Survey," *Cision PR Newswire*, May 24, 2016, https://www.prnewswire.com/news-releases/volatility-disruption-driving-growth-strategies-ma-transformation-in-energy-sector-kpmg-survey-300274156.html
11. Julia Pyper, "Electric Utilities Prepare for a Grid Dominated by Renewable Energy," *Green Tech Media*, June 16, 2016, https://www.greentechmedia.com/articles/read/the-electric-industry-prepares-for-a-renewable-energy-dominant-grid#gs.7qu2gs.
12. Jacques Leslie, "Utilities Grapple with Rooftop Solar and the New Energy Landscape," *YaleEnvironment360*, August 31, 2017, https://e360.yale.edu/features/utilities-grapple-with-rooftop-solar-and-the-new-energy-landscape.
13. Amy Zipkin, "Airports Are Losing Money as Ride-Hailing Services Grow," *New York Times*, December 11, 2017, https://www.nytimes.com/2017/12/11/business/airports-ride-hailing-services.html.

14. Rosie Spinks, "Your Uber or Lyft Ride Could Be the Reason American Airports Get Worse," *Quartz*, November 21, 2018, https://qz.com/1471712/your-uber-or-lyft-ride-could-be-the-reason-american-airports-get-worse/.
15. Ibid.
16. Airport Urbanism, "What's the Future of Parking," *Airport-Urbanism.com*, September 14, 2018, https://airporturbanism.com/articles/whats-the-future-of-parking.
17. Zipkin, "Airports Are Losing Money."
18. Ibid.
19. Ibid.
20. Postmates homepage. 2019, https://postmates.com/.
21. Biz Carson, "The Amazon-Whole Foods Deal Could Have Killed Instacart. Instead, The Startup Is Stronger Than Ever." *Forbes*, December 12, 2017. https://www.forbes.com/sites/bizcarson/2017/11/08/amazon-whole-foods-deal-future-of-instacart-grocery-delivery/#6e79e30b6d5a.
22. Instacart, "Instacart: About," *LinkedIn*, 2019, https://www.linkedin.com/company/instacart/about/.
23. Kate Clark, "Postmates Lines Up Another $100M Ahead of IPO," *Tech Crunch*, February, 2019, https://techcrunch.com/2019/01/10/postmates-lines-up-another-100m-ahead-of-ipo/.
24. Jillian D'Onfro, "The Founder Of A Dot-Com Disaster Is Giving His Old Grocery Delivery Idea Another Shot," *Business Insider*, April 18, 2014, https://www.businessinsider.com/louis-borders-webvan-founder-hds-2014–4.
25. Carol Emert, "Venture Lessons in Webvan Collapse/Financing History a Cautionary Tale," *San Francisco Chronicle*, July 15, 2001, https://www.sfgate.com/bayarea/article/Venture-lessons-in-Webvan-collapse-Financing-2899418.php.

26. Matt Richtel, "Webvan Stock Price Closes 65% Above Initial Offering," *New York Times*, November 6, 1999, https://www.nytimes.com/1999/11/06/business/webvan-stock-price-closes-65-above-initial-offering.html.
27. Ibid.
28. Ray Delgado, "Webvan Goes Under/Online Grocer Shuts Down—$830 Million Lost, 2,000 Workers Fired," *San Francisco Chronicle*, July 9, 2001, https://www.sfgate.com/news/article/Webvan-goes-under-Online-grocer-shuts-down-2901586.php.
29. Nate Lanxon, "The Greatest Defunct Web Sites and Dotcom Disasters," *CNet*, November 18, 2009, https://www.cnet.com/news/the-greatest-defunct-web-sites-and-dotcom-disasters/.
30. FMI and Nielsen, "Digital Shopper," *fmi.org*, 2019, https://www.fmi.org/digital-shopper/.
31. Leadership Network, "Innovation the Dyson Way," *TheLeadershipNetwork.com*, November 17, 2016, https://theleadershipnetwork.com/article/innovation-dyson-reimagining-appliances.
32. Leadership Network, "Innovation the Dyson Way."
33. Carroll Gantz, *The Vacuum Cleaner: A History* (Jefferson, NC: Mcfarland & Company, 2012), p. 44.
34. Bloomberg, "Inventor James Dyson Now UK's Wealthiest Person after Dyson Vacuum Cleaner Firm Cleans Up," *South China Morning Post: International Edition*, January 23, 2019, https://www.scmp.com/magazines/style/people-events/article/2183307/inventor-james-dyson-now-uks-wealthiest-person-after.
35. Gabriel Rozenberg and Sarah Butler, "Dyson Knighted in New Year's Honours List," *Times*, December 30, 2006, https://www.thetimes.co.uk/article/dyson-knighted-in-new-years-honours-list-533wzdg8pb9.

36. Leadership Network, "Innovation the Dyson Way."
37. Dyson, Dyson.com, 2019.
38. Julien Petit, "The Dyson Mindset = "Everything Can Improve," *Medium*, February 26, 2018, https://medium.com/@julien99/the-dyson-mindset-everything-can-improve-36191f2cd63.

# Chapter 5

## The Lonely Innovator Myth

In popular culture and historical narratives, a myth persists about the "lonely inventor," toiling night and day until he or she comes up with an idea so perfect that it spits in the face of convention, blows everyone's minds, and becomes a near overnight sensation, changing the world as we know it. Alexander Graham Bell and the telephone, Samuel F. B. Morse and the telegraph, jazz-hating Thomas Edison and the light bulb—we often think of such luminaries as the great inventors of yesterday, from whom so many modern conveniences and technologies were born before being adopted en masse and spread throughout the world.

But that's not exactly how it happens. In reality, Bell didn't invent the phone. He actually filed for the patent—before he had even been able to get his invention to work—on the same day that a guy named Elisha Gray did.[1] Morse wasn't the only one to develop the telegraph in the 1800s; two English scientists actually filed for a British patent of a similar machine before Morse did so in the US, and before his famous public demonstration of the telegraph in January 1838.[2] And good ol' Tom Edison didn't invent the light bulb at all—incandescent bulbs already existed before he figured out that a type of bamboo would act as a better filament than what was then being used.[3]

What truly led to these three men's success was that they had the necessary support to take "their" inventions to the next level.

Bell had his assistant Thomas Watson, and he joined with others to create the Bell Patent Association, which later turned into the Bell Telephone Company.[4] In the 1870s and 1880s, the company's patent was called into question and a case was brought against them, initiated by the Western Union telegraph company, which turned into a lengthy legal, multi-case battle known as the Telephone Cases. After the case made it all the way up to the US Supreme Court, Bell's patent was upheld by a four-to-three vote.[5] If he hadn't had the company (and their lawyers) by his side, he could easily have lost the case. Morse had help in the form of his colleague Alfred Vail, who worked tirelessly to improve Morse's design.[6] Edison's real invention, and arguably a more important one in the long run, may have been the establishment of the first industrial research lab ever, which he set up in Menlo Park, New Jersey.[7] There he joined forces with a team of other scientists and inventors to put his ideas into practice, including that bamboo filament.

Then there's Henry Ford, the father of the first mass-produced, affordable automobile, the Model T. He's no different than Bell, Edison, or Morse. After failing with two car companies, his third, which he started in 1903, found success, even though he, like Bell, ran into some patent issues of his own. Before Ford's Model T, a patent on the automobile was registered in 1895 to George Selden, which set off a chain of events that would lead to Selden selling the rights to his Electric Vehicle Company, which was then later licensed by the new Association of Licensed Automobile Manufacturers in 1903.[8] Ford applied for a "Selden license" and was denied, but he moved forward with production anyway, causing him to be sued.

However, Ford won the case—the Selden patent was found to relate only to cars with certain specifications—and his business took off, but only with the assistance of his company, engineers, and eventually all of the factory workers who made mass production possible. (One historical side note is that Selden's original vehicle was electric, whereas Ford's employed the gas engine. One hundred years later, it seems that Selden's ghost lives on, with the likes of Elon Musk, one of the best-known innovators of today, now attempting to bring electric cars to the masses.)

Alone, all of these men were mere inventors—collaborating with others made them innovators. Their names wouldn't be known in history as they are today if it weren't for the aid they had from colleagues and team members to bring their ideas to life and then to market and sell their products far and wide (not to mention handle all their legal patent cases). The catalyst of any innovation is typically an individual, the spark that leads to something new. But the fire would go out if it weren't for a team that supports the individual and his or her ideas. Individuals can be inventors, coming up with novel, original products or services. Hidden in a garage or a lab somewhere, there's most definitely an eccentric visionary contemplating the next "big thing" (whether or not this "thing" comes to fruition is another matter). But despite having the greatest ideas in the world, without a team an idea remains just an idea, no matter how groundbreaking it might be. You may have the right innovation mindset and attitude, but without others you're going to go nowhere. Even filing a patent requires collaborating with somebody else.

But for some reason, just like the "lonely inventor," a misconception of the "lonely innovator" persists, as if one person should be the sole proprietor of the concept, tasked with "innovating." Not only would that be overwhelming, but it would also accomplish nothing. Simply said, solo innovation does not exist—it's a team sport. Working in solitude may lead to invention, but not innovation, because it requires collaboration with others. Innovation only happens thanks to groups of people working together to achieve specific goals. Innovation is at its best when it's a result of collaboration by inclusive, diverse, cross-functional teams that are empowered to make decisions and enact change. As a leader, it's your job to create an environment where teams like these can emerge and succeed.

## Treat Innovation Like a Team Sport

Despite popular belief, invention is not the same as innovation. Just as people confuse disruption with innovation, they get invention, ideation, and innovation all twisted up into one singular concept. They are related, but the distinction is quite simple: invention and ideation are all about coming up with ideas, innovation is about *executing* on them. To put it in relevant business terms, invention does not require commercial success, but innovation can't exist without it. Whether innovators develop an idea from scratch or build on successes of the past, they must execute continuously and relentlessly, which is really the only thing that is under their control when it comes to success anyhow. Inventors, on the other hand, can create something, then call it a day.

Consider the number of patents filed every year with the United States Patent and Trademark Office, which receives applications for literally hundreds of thousands of them.[9] In 2018, they issued their ten millionth—they've been busy since Bell, Morse, Edison, and Ford.[10] The year prior, 3.2 million patents were applied for globally.[11] Many of those patents will never be acted upon—that's invention, not innovation. Of course, many inventions are not patented and are kept as trade secrets, like Coca-Cola's recipe, and some patent activity occurs for other reasons besides commercialization, like image and prestige, not to mention patent trolling. But 97 percent of all US patents never end up making *any* money, probably because most inventors lack the skills to take their ideas to the market.[12] That's where teams come into play.

Teams are absolutely necessary to figure out whether certain ideas are worth pursuing in the first place, providing insight into their viability (most team members will appreciate their peers' help with this aspect early on). If they are viable, then working together in teams is the only way to turn these good ideas into reality. Otherwise they'll never come to fruition. Still, teams will only be successful if they consist of individuals with unique skills, personalities, and backgrounds and who are willing to collaborate, regardless of title or function.

Related to this is the idea that no function or team within an organization should have a monopoly on innovation—not now and not ever. In fact, it's quite dangerous if only one does. Transformative ideas can occur anywhere, and their scope should not be limited to an employee's core function or job description. As a leader, it is not your responsibility to "box" your people in, but rather to give them opportunities to explore innovation while helping them to align their efforts with organizational goals. Help them express their ideas and subsequently move beyond ideation and invention. Have them start innovating by connecting them with other employees who are open to the possibilities of innovation and willing to work with cross-functional teams. Effective, cross-functional teams are essential to solving one of the biggest problems hurting even the most successful companies and making it impossible for them to innovate—the dreaded silo mentality.

### Beware of Silos

If you've ever worked in an office—and if you're reading this book you probably have—then you've most likely run into the silo mentality on more than one occasion. Maybe you've been guilty of it yourself once or twice, sometimes without even realizing it. This mentality is a mindset in which employees of different divisions or departments within the same organization do not share information outside of their own immediate group, even if it would benefit everyone in the organization overall. This situation creates "information silos," in which ideas are not exchanged freely or openly.

Sometimes these silos occur because people believe projects or activities run faster when they don't involve others. Employees may also keep certain information for themselves for their own benefit or for the benefit of their team. Other times, this mentality is built in at the management level, with managers from different areas competing with one another. No matter how it originates, whether from personal politics or perceived higher purpose, the silo mentality has been credited with creating low morale, impeding a productive company culture,[13] reducing efficiency, and killing off innovation.[14] And if information isn't shared, then of course joint strategy, metrics, and transparency go right out the window. Not good at all.

When any of these results present themselves, leaders start looking around for the culprit, but often overlook information silos. This blind spot is in part due to the fact that silos were actually relied upon for years, especially in areas like research and development. Some teams also still need silos due to the highly specialized nature of certain fields, sensitive information, and company secrets, for example, in the pharmaceutical or defense industries. This approach is understandable in such settings, but aside from these special circumstances, such a mentality is out of date and unnecessary for most organizations. And looking to the past, it's easy to see that even then this mindset created some major issues. The development of the digital Sony Walkman succinctly illustrates how this silo mentality can go wrong.

Sony was still kicking ass and taking names at the head of the technology innovation pack in the 1990s, after having hit a homerun with the Walkman in 1979—that's right, the pre-streaming, pre-digital, pre-compact-disc, portable analog cassette tape player. As the company grew throughout the '80s and '90s, growing pains ensued, and management decided to chop Sony up into twenty-five different subcompanies, which inevitably created twenty-five different divisions, and, you guessed it, twenty-five individual silos.[15] Come 1999, Sony decided to up its game by releasing a new digital Walkman in response to digital music adoption. The only problem was that more than one division within the company had been developing such a product. As a result, Sony released two different digital Walkman devices, each using different proprietary technology, on the same day,[16] which were shortly followed by a *third* version.[17] This situation confused customers, not to mention Sony's salespeople and retailers, to no end.

Sony was so fragmented that its left hand pretty much didn't know what its right hand was doing. As anthropologist Gillian Tett explains in *The Silo Effect,* the different digital music players were developed separately and were not "widely compatible."[18] She writes, "None of these departments, or silos, was able to agree on a single product approach, or even communicate with each other to swap ideas, or agree on a joint strategy."[19] No wonder many companies have tried to abandon the silo mentality in recent years. Unfortunately, it still persists.

Large organizations are especially prone to silos due to their size and political nature. This may come from different department leaders gunning for the same promotion, believing that they are at odds for one reason or another, or having some agenda that they think they'll be unable to achieve if they "give away" certain information. When an organization is small—a startup for example—silos are less likely to exist. There is an inherently cooperative environment in which everyone works together toward a common goal and they know silos would only hurt them. As startups grow, however, silos tend to form, especially as these small companies turn into large corporations. The challenge is therefore to avoid the silo mentality no matter the size of the organization or its rate of growth.

The issue is not just that the silo mentality produces these silos of information, but it also produces mental silos, building walls that block the sharing of knowledge and ideas. It's bad enough that data or other information may not be making its way between departments, but when employees stop putting their heads together to develop solutions to problems or otherwise innovate, our mortal enemy stagnation starts to sneak in once again. By supporting cross-functional teams, leaders can put a stop to this silo mentality before it begins. It all comes down to working together toward a common goal.

### Tear Down the Walls

Teams are all about skills and personalities, not territory. When it comes to innovation, cross-functional teams lead to the best outcomes as they work across departments, disrupting the silo mentality and sharing ideas and information that may have otherwise been left unexplored. Think of the process almost as a form of crowdsourcing, in which you pull in employees who hold different positions, roles, and ranks within your organization to create the best team possible. In doing so, more employees, and leaders too, will get excited about innovation as it begins to spread throughout the organization.

Team members all need to buy in to the prospects for success. You can have all the executive support in the world, but if the members of your teams don't believe in the power of innovation, they're not going to make it central to their thinking, processes, or performance. Therefore, just as you drive strategy (discussed in Chapter 2), you must lead by example, provide support, and set your team up for success.

Working cross-functionally may seem daunting to some, and that's entirely understandable. In almost any organization, everything is a political process, especially in large companies. Departments are so separated, they tend to block one another, claiming ownership over an idea or task that should really be the domain of all teams. Many employees are content to stick with their tight-knit group, pay attention to the politics and nuances of their department alone, and try to just eek it out until 5 pm. It's sad but true. Innovation does not work in a bureaucratic or political environment; it's a mindset that can't just sit with one team alone. If it does, it will never become a part of the fabric of the culture. Simply said, innovation belongs to all.

Those of us who work cross-functionally every day (typically middle managers) understand that in order to survive, drive growth, stay in power, or influence outcomes, we need to create value for all stakeholders. We can only do so if we first get all of our employees on board. If we don't work cross-functionally, this will be impossible. In fact, we won't be able to accomplish anything, especially in a large organization, since at the end of the day, in order to execute, we must have everyone behind us or aligned with us, and they must all have a valued role in the process. By working in such a cross-functional manner, we become greater than the sum of our parts.

Opening up and working cross-functionally supports co-innovation and allows us all to take a hand in the success of our companies' initiatives and results. Restricting innovation to any one group is counterproductive. Innovation is about every single function, and so it should be balanced within those functions and across them. Interdepartmental work breaks down silos and contributes to a more productive, innovative culture. This cross-functional approach also helps in developing greater diversity and inclusion among teams, which is paramount to any organization's success in driving strategy and reaching goals. Combining people from various backgrounds who've had different life experiences, both personal and professional, offers a mix of skills, expertise, and knowledge that creates stronger teams.

## Foster Diversity and Inclusion

Innovation is always better together. Its possibilities are greater and stronger if we are able to tackle complexity as a group, not just as single individuals. But if we all come from the same background, we're all likely to propose similar solutions to any given problem. We're even likely to miss the problem to begin with. Different points of view should be encouraged because they are essential to progress. This means we won't agree all the time, but dissent is good—it breathes life into conversations, ideas, and plans. These different points of view can only come from a diverse team, meaning we still maintain our individuality but work together toward a common vision. In that way, our teams are strengthened through our experiences.

Diversity provides different frames of reference to find solutions and create value for a wider customer market. Inclusion makes sure that all of our diverse voices are heard, ideas considered, and strategies incorporated as appropriate. Even if we have the most diverse staff on the planet, it doesn't matter if we only listen to a small, homogenous segment of it. Similarly, if we've developed a culture that does not support diversity, inclusion will be impossible. If we allow everyone to be heard, however, as our teams work together toward a common goal, we'll see an undeniable impact.

Of course, diversity isn't based solely on our professional experience, though that's important as well, but on who we are, where we're from, and how we grew up. A group that is racially, socially, and culturally diverse—including different genders, ages, abilities, ethnicities, and educations—creates more opportunities for innovation. In such an environment, we all have the chance to gain insight and understanding about the immediate problem we're trying to solve, and about the world in which we live. Most importantly, we have the opportunity to share these ideas with others. In this way, as our business grows, so do we as people.

As a leader, maybe diversity is not one of your top goals and you're more concerned about impact metrics, but don't let that blind you from the facts. Hard evidence shows that diverse teams perform better. A 2018 finding by Great Place to Work, a business consultant that conducts employee surveys and provides "great place to work" certifications, showed that organizations that involve every employee have higher levels of innovation. Based on a study of nearly 800 companies across numerous industries and around 50,000 employees, it was found "that organizations in which everyone participates in generating new ideas, products, and services speed past their rivals and adjust rapidly to changing market conditions."[20] Great Place to Work also reported that such a culture will "generate more high-quality ideas, realize greater speed in implementation, and achieve greater agility—resulting in 5.5 times the revenue growth of peers with a less inclusive approach to innovation."[21] Now that's an impact metric worth noting!

Similar results have been found elsewhere as well. A 2017 report by Boston Consulting Group found "companies that reported above-average diversity on their management teams also reported innovation revenue that was 19 percentage points higher than that of companies with below-average leadership diversity—45% of total revenue versus just 26%."[22]

According to research by the McKinsey consulting company, diversity actually creates a competitive advantage: "Companies in the top quartile for racial and ethnic diversity are 35 percent more likely to have financial returns above their respective national industry medians."[23] Gender diversity shows a similar trend, with companies in the top quartile being "15 percent more likely to have financial returns above their respective national industry medians."[24] Similarly, students from racially and socioeconomically diverse schools perform better, with higher average test scores, greater college enrollment, an enhancement in leadership skills, and improved intellectual self-confidence.[25] Diverse working and learning environments also create more productive, effective, and creative teams.[26] As we interact with people from various backgrounds we learn how to anticipate different viewpoints and work toward consensus.[27]

And if that's not enough proof, as reported by *Scientific American*, decades of research by professionals from numerous, varied fields—including economists, psychologists, demographers, sociologists, and organizational scientists—show that groups that exhibit social diversity are *more innovative* than homogenous ones.[28] Need I say more?

Still, many businesses have yet to get the memo. McKinsey also reported that no industry or company is in the top quartile on both gender diversity and ethnic and racial diversity.[29] Women remain underrepresented in top corporate positions throughout the world, and 97 percent of US companies do not have senior-leadership teams that reflect the demographic composition of America's population and labor force.[30] Seems like it might be up to us innovators to push the envelope here.

The reality is that most leaders tend to be surrounded by people who think and act the same way, even when there's a perception of diversity. Innovation, however, comes from actual diversity in thought, which is a result of different life and professional experiences. When it comes down to doing the hard work of innovation, diversity is the single biggest element that separates good ideas from not so good ones and accelerates execution to the max. As a leader, you're developing these diverse teams and connections across the organization, but it's impossible to do so without a solid partnership with HR.

### Partner with HR

Innovation is all about talent, and so is HR. It's only natural that the two go hand in hand. Unfortunately, a lot of leaders don't recognize this fact. Instead, many see HR's only job as preventing litigation and handling employee disputes. Though these are important aspects of the HR teams' duties, they are certainly not the only ones. Equally important is their focus on talent and culture, which they enable through recruiting, hiring, and onboarding the best employees. It surprises many people when I tell them that since that's such an integral part of their role, HR is actually a key driver of innovation.

Today, HR is transitioning from a policy-centric entity to a people-centric one, focusing more directly on talent and employee experiences. That's why the term "Chief People Officer" is emerging. In one way or another, HR is the only group that has a connection with every single employee (or potential employee) in an organization, so their team leaders often have information that other leaders don't. They are also typically the first to recognize the changes taking place across the entire ecosystem. Think about it: they have the opportunity to connect with people of all different levels, across geographies and industries. Since HR is tasked with picking the best candidates for the future, they also have first-hand knowledge of employee expectations, desires, skills, and capabilities, which contributes to their unique insights into industry trends and evolving markets.

We live in a knowledge-based economy, where talent is often more essential than capital. Of course techno-futurists, and many regular folks you run into on the street, fear that robots are taking away our jobs (by the way, when was the last time you saw a robot just walking around your office?), but until that *Singularity* moment when robots become self-aware, our economy and work life will remain rooted in *human* knowledge and professions. In many industries there is a lot of available capital but not a lot of talent, particularly with the right skills. To put this into perspective, US unemployment is at its lowest since 2000, and nearly 60 percent of employers (did you read that clearly, *employers*), struggle to fill job vacancies within twelve weeks.[31] Expect things to get worse: according to the management consulting company Korn Ferry, "A major crisis is looming over organizations and economies throughout the world. By 2030, demand for skilled workers will outstrip supply, resulting in a global talent shortage of more than 85.2 million people."[32]

Without talent, you don't have anyone to innovate; no employees equals no work. Now, this is not my "workers unite and take over" moment, but it should be obvious to anyone running an organization that top talent is essential to building great teams, and, as discussed, diverse, cross-functional teams lead to true innovation. Without HR, it's impossible to find, develop, and retain the right employees. It's also impossible to educate your workforce and help them develop skills that will contribute not only to their personal success but to the organization's success as well. Innovation mindsets need to be cultivated companywide, but that can't take place if you've got less than stellar players on your team. Innovation is about people and the talent and experiences they bring to the table. In this way, HR has a major hand in fostering diversity and inclusion and facilitating innovation throughout the organization, creating a culture of openness and respect for others' points of view.

And innovation is a concept used by HR to attract and keep the best talent today. In fact, the opportunity to innovate is considered one of the key aspects that's driving employee satisfaction and retention. In a 2018 survey, 42 percent of millennials and 47 percent of Gen Xers stated that they'd leave their current jobs not just for increased compensation, but also for a "more innovative environment."[33] Now, what each employee means by "innovation" is likely quite different from person to person, but it's all based around having the chance to unleash their inner creativity to generate better value.

That better value can be customer experience, faster execution, new products, or, for some, kombucha on tap in the cafeteria. Whatever that value may be, it must be identified because it will empower employees and lead them to grow and innovate. So, don't be scared to start small—kombucha on tap for all! And if that's hard to supply, you might need to rethink your actions. (Seriously, if your employees aren't empowered to change the menu in your cafeteria, you probably don't have the right environment to solve a customer problem.)

As "Chief People Officers," HR's leaders and team members help ensure that their people—that is, everyone in the organization—have the chance to be heard. If all voices aren't shared equally, great teams will be impossible to create. By hearing everyone out, HR sets the tone of the organization's culture, defining its core values through its people and helping them work together cross-functionally, across silos, to ensure that these values are understood. Without HR's help in creating diverse teams willing to work together, innovation would never be possible.

## Case Study: Cisco

Cisco is a 50-billion-dollar company that has powered most of the technologies that have made the Internet what it is today. One of the key components of the company's success is that its leaders realize Cisco's strength is not contingent on technology, but on its employees and the value they produce for their customers. At Cisco, I've had the luck and good fortune to experience what happens when employees break free from silos and work together cross-functionally in diverse and inclusive teams. I truly believe that Cisco's innovate everywhere challenge and their Our People Deal are the perfect examples of teams working together to innovate and produce real results. The Our People Deal slogan ("Connect Everything. Innovate Everywhere. Benefit Everyone.") is built into the company's culture at every level, creating unprecedented value for customers and the world at large.

For a number of years, I ran startup engagement programs for Cisco. In that time, the programs evolved, but the goal was always the same: collaborate with startups to discover new business opportunities and execute on them together for a mutual win-win relationship. Every year that I ran the program, Cisco employees would call me and say they too had ideas they thought were worthwhile, and asked if they could be a part of the program as well. Unfortunately, I always had to tell them no:

since they were employees of Cisco, they didn't qualify. Eventually, one of our employees pointed out the absurdity in this rationale: "So you're saying," she asked, "that if I have a valuable idea and I want to share it with the company, I have to quit, then partner with someone else or form my own startup, and only then can I come back to you to potentially gain the company's support?"

I was left speechless. She was totally right—we were paying more attention to ideas coming from startups than those coming from our own employees. Cisco certainly had amazing ways for employees to bring their ideas forward, but I realized this was mostly happening in technology organizations, such as Engineering. Nearly half of the company was left out. Something had to be done.

My team and I partnered with HR and Employee Communications to conduct a series of focus groups across the company. We discovered that an overwhelming majority of employees were eager to innovate but were unclear on the pathways for successfully nurturing new ideas to execution. Many employees felt that they had good ideas that would result in better company performance, but they had no one to take them to, since innovation was not in the "scope of their function." They needed support, time, space, and money to foster and implement their best ideas for new ventures. In particular, they wanted a central forum where they could explain new ideas, build them out with colleagues, and present them to executives and decision makers. That's when my colleague Mathilde Durvy and I decided to roll up our sleeves and work across Cisco to redefine innovation. Our goal was simple: empower every single employee to innovate with a meaningful difference. Easy, right?

As a first step in this journey, we gathered every leader in charge of departmental innovation programs in the company; there were over fifty at the time. When we all got into the same room, it was obvious that neither our goals nor our strategy were aligned—we were operating in silos. The good news was that almost everyone in the room wanted to change that. Over the next two days, we discussed the challenges we were facing and how we could all work together to move forward. It was obvious that we shared similar problems and wanted the same outcomes.

*(continued)*

## Case Study: Cisco (*continued*)

We got on the same page and established processes, agreeing to keep each other informed, reduce duplication of efforts, and, most importantly, support one another to make our programs more impactful. Together, we decided to roll out a unified innovation program available to all employees of Cisco, regardless of their function, job title, or location.

Thanks to the enthusiastic support from our CEO Chuck Robbins and our Chief People Officer Fran Katsoudas, we built a replicable companywide process for innovation focused on supporting both ideation and execution. Our goal was three-fold:

- Capture disruptive venture ideas from employees and help them grow.
- Develop entrepreneurship skills and culture across Cisco.
- Enhance employee experience and collaboration.

We then proceeded in four phases modeled after the lifecycle of startups: ideate, validate, fund, and build.

In the ideate phase, all employees were invited to propose a solution to a major problem or opportunity facing Cisco. They created or joined a cross-functional team to post their ideas on a collaborative platform visible to all employees. A panel of judges—as well as employee voting—narrowed these entries down to fifteen semifinalists, who advanced to the validate phase. From there, the semifinalist teams had three months to work with mentors and coaches to validate the user desirability, technical feasibility, and business viability of their idea. They distilled these into an investor pitch and business model canvas. Executives chose five of the six finalist teams; employees selected the other finalist through online voting.

The third phase was funding, in which the six finalists had three weeks to find internal sponsors and harness support for their venture. At the end of this phase, they gave a live pitch to a panel of internal and external industry leaders, laying out the case for their ideas and responding to questions from the panel. The three winners of the challenge were announced at an all-company meeting, and then moved onto the fourth phase—building. In this phase, each winning team received $25,000 in seed funding,

$25,000 as recognition, and the option to enter a three-month innovation rotation program to give them space to develop their venture. Each team also received a corporate concierge for help with practical affairs as well as assistance from Cisco leaders in determining the most appropriate next steps.

As the program has evolved—as of 2019 it was entering its fifth year—we have invested in giving our employees clearer guidance in the areas in which the company needs to innovate the most. They can still pick whatever projects they want, but we're helping to drive their efforts and keep them engaged, making sure that their ideas can be executed; remember, without execution innovation is just invention. The program therefore develops more than just inventors, supporting innovators throughout the company too. The concept of "companywide" is very important to the process, so everyone involved must work in cross-functional teams as well. As we always explain, without such teams, there is no diversity, no new ways of considering concepts or ideas, and there's no way of succeeding.

Employee ideas continue to be judged by peers, not just executives. Each idea is published, meaning it's visible to all, and it is reviewed by all levels of employees, some as high up as directors and some who are interns, but they are all part of a diverse group who can look at the ideas from varying perspectives, bringing in their own insights as well. For all the ideas that we do not advance forward, we maintain transparency by explaining specifically what's lacking, and what needs to be developed.

Through this process, we learn what employees care about and connect them with other people from around the world. We also break down organizational silos and create a diverse community of collaborators across teams. The innovation program has developed into one of the industry's best, and most replicable, of its kind, spanning 75,000 employees across 247 Cisco offices in 96 countries. Just as important for Cisco's future success has been the change in the company's culture: employees now have the opportunity and support to propose new products, services, and process improvements and see themselves as innovators, no matter their position or function. We've succeeded in creating an environment and culture of innovation that is second to none, all due to teams working together to innovate toward amazing results.

## Summary: Innovation Is a Team Sport

The last thing we want to do is confuse invention with innovation. You can "invent" and "ideate" by yourself all day and night, but innovation is a team effort that requires execution. To that end, innovative teams are more important than a lonely inventor, or innovator, and need to be supported. But innovation can't take place in just one team, or under the domain of just one group—it must be opened up to all employees across ranks and departments. As a leader, if you want to be successful, never do it alone. Cash in some political capital and go against company norms to bring everyone together, break down silos, and work cross-functionally. By doing so, you'll be sharing in the fun, passion, knowledge, and pursuit of new ideas that make innovation such a gratifying experience.

And by "everyone," I don't mean a homogenous group that's just going to spin their wheels with the same old ideas. The best teams are inclusive and diverse as they bring a broader perspective to the table and develop stronger innovative solutions. We need diverse, inclusive teams that look at the world in different ways and can provide insights that lead to personal and professional growth for team members, and top- and bottom-line growth for the organization overall (don't forget your activity and impact metrics!).

HR plays the most critical role in creating strong, diverse teams across departments, and hiring and cultivating talent that will be able to work cross-functionally. By developing talent and providing opportunities, HR becomes the key driver of innovation. Looking for the skills, not just filling the functions, proves to be invaluable. Still, innovation must be supported throughout the organization instead of resting with one team, or person, alone. Working cross-functionally helps expand the possibilities and avoid this potential problem. Innovating across functions is imperative, as it gets everyone excited and on board the innovation train, but as you'll see in Chapter 6, once this starts taking place between different companies and organizations, that's when things start to get really good.

### Principle

Diverse inclusive teams are the lifeblood of innovation, which can't take place without them.

### Action

- Make a concerted effort to break down silos through cross-functional teams.
- Maintain a focus on executable ideas—think innovation, not invention.
- Partner with your HR organization to help develop strong teams, collaborate across functions, and create an inclusive culture where everyone is welcome.

### Obstacles

A lack of diversity and inclusion and lack of an open culture lead to a stifling of ideas and voices. The silo mentality affects leaders and employees, especially in larger organizations, contributing to little shared knowledge, duplication of efforts, and subpar execution.

### Outcome

Innovation is enabled through cross-functional teams, made up of individuals with diverse backgrounds and expertise, that openly exchange information, believe in the value of collaboration, and work together to get things done.

## Notes

1. Mark A. Lemley, "The Myth of the Sole Inventor," Stanford Public Law Working Paper No. 1856610, June 2, 2011, https://papers.ssrn.com/sol3/papers.cfm?abstract_id=1856610.
2. Barbara Maranzani, "6 Things You May Not Know About Samuel Morse," *History.com*, August 22, 2018, https://www.history.com/news/six-things-you-may-not-know-about-samuel-morse.

3. Derek Thompson, "Forget Edison: This Is How History's Greatest Inventions Really Happened," *Atlantic*, June 15, 2012, https://www.theatlantic.com/business/archive/2012/06/forget-edison-this-is-how-historys-greatest-inventions-really-happened/258525/.

4. Louis Galambos, "Theodore N. Vail and the Role of Innovation in the Modern Bell System," *Business History Review* 66, (no. 1, Spring 1992), https://www.jstor.org/stable/3117054.

5. Christopher Beauchamp, *Invented by Law: Alexander Graham Bell and the Patent That Chanted America* (Cambridge, MA: Harvard University Press, 2015), https://www.jstor.org/stable/j.ctt13x0h8z.

6. Courtney Bellizzi, "A Forgotten History: Alfred Vail and Samuel Morse," *Smithsonian Institution Archives,* May 24, 2011, https://siarchives.si.edu/blog/forgotten-history-alfred-vail-and-samuel-morse.

7. Vernon Trollinger, "Happy Birthday, Thomas Edison!" *Bounce Energy Blog*, February 11, 2013, https://www.bounceenergy.com/blog/2013/02/happy-birthday-thomas-edison/.

8. Nigel Ravenhill, "Famous Patent Wars: 1900–1950," *IP Folio Blog*, 2019, http://blog.ipfolio.com/famous-patent-wars-1900–1950.

9. United States Patent and Trademark Office, "U.S. Patent Activity, Calendar Years 1790 to the Present," USPTO.gov, 2019, https://www.uspto.gov/web/offices/ac/ido/oeip/taf/h_counts.htm.

10. Nilay Patel, "The US Patent Office has issues 10 million patents," *Verge*, June 19, 2018, https://www.theverge.com/2018/6/19/17478898/uspto-utility-patents-10-million-issued.

11. WIPO, "IP Facts and Figures: Patents and Utility Models," *wipo.int*, 2019. https://www.wipo.int/edocs/infogdocs/en/ipfactsandfigures2018/.

12. Stephen Key, "97 Percent of All Patents Never Make Any Money," *All Business*, 2019, https://www.allbusiness.com/97-percent-of-all-patents-never-make-any-money-15258080–1.html.

13. Business Dictionary, "Silo Mentality," *BusinessDictionary.com*, http://www.businessdictionary.com/definition/silo-mentality.html.

14. Will Kenton (Reviewer), "Silo Mentality," *Investopedia*, June 25, 2019 (updated), https://www.investopedia.com/terms/s/silo-mentality.asp.

15. Jeff Boss, "Silos Are Killing Amazon's Potential. Don't Let Them Kill Yours," *Forbes*, September 18, 2017, https://www.forbes.com/sites/jeffboss/2017/09/18/silos-are-killing-amazons-potential-dont-let-them-kill-yours/#6dfe24745fbc.

16. Ibid.

17. Gillian Tett, "Why the Silo Effect Makes Us Stupid," *Financial Review*, August 28, 2015, https://www.afr.com/lifestyle/arts-and-entertainment/books/the—big-walkman-switchoff-how-silos-stifle-progress-in-the-digital-age-20150824-gj64kk.

18. Gillian Tett, *The Silo Effect: The Peril of Expertise and the Promise of Breaking Down Barriers* (New York: Simon & Schuster, 2016).

19. Ibid.

20. Great Place to Work, "Innovation By All," *greatplacetowork.com,* 2018, https://www.greatplacetowork.com/resources/blog/innovation-by-all-better-all-around.

21. Ibid.

22. Rocío Lorenzo, Nicole Voigt, Miki Tsusaka, Matt Krentz, and Katie Abouzahr, "How Diverse Leadership Teams Boost Innovation," *BCG.com*, January 23, 2018, https://www.bcg.com/en-us/publications/2018/how-diverse-leadership-teams-boost-innovation.aspx.

23. Vivian Hunt, Dennis Layton, and Sara Prince, "Why Diversity Matters," *McKinsey.com*, January 2015, https://www.mckinsey.com/business-functions/organization/our-insights/why-diversity-matters.
24. Ibid.
25. Century Foundation, "The Benefits of Socioeconomically and Racially Integrated Schools and Classrooms," *TCF.org*, April 29, 2019, https://tcf.org/content/facts/the-benefits-of-socioeconomically-and-racially-integrated-schools-and-classrooms/?session=1&session=1.
26. Ibid.
27. Ibid.
28. Katherine W. Phillips, "How Diversity Makes Us Smarter," *Scientific American,* October 1, 2014, https://www.scientificamerican.com/article/how-diversity-makes-us-smarter/.
29. Hunt, Layton, and Prince, "Why Diversity Matters."
30. Ibid.
31. Career Builder, "The Skills Gap Is Costing Companies Nearly $1 Million Annually, According to New CareerBuilder Survey," *Career Builder: Press Room*, April 13, 2017, http://press.careerbuilder.com/2017–04–13-The-Skills-Gap-Is-Costing-Companies-Nearly-1-Million-Annually-According-to-New-CareerBuilder-Survey.
32. Korn Ferry, "The Global Talent Crunch: Introduction," *Future of Work*, 2018, https://futureofwork.kornferry.com/introduction/.
33. Alex Goryachev, "Winning the Talent War: How Innovation Attracts and Retains Employees," *HR Drive*, May 31, 2018, https://www.hrdive.com/news/winning-the-talent-war-how-innovation-attracts-and-retains-employees/524662/.

# Chapter 6

## Innovation Wants to Be Free

Though the idea of open source began in the 1970s, the movement itself didn't gain much mainstream notoriety until around 2001, the year that Steve Ballmer, the CEO of Microsoft at the time, called open-source software, specifically Linux, a "cancer."[1] Linux, started by Linus Torvalds in the 1990s, was an "open-source" computer operating system, one that made corporate America nervous and a lot of software developers and computer scientists excited. Open source is both a description of a type of computer software and a philosophy, in which the freedom to share information is valued above all else—in this case computer code and free programs that can be developed, built upon, improved, and redistributed.

It all began with the Internet, born as a project funded by the US Department of Defense that quickly moved into the domain of academia, an environment in which a free sharing of knowledge and ideas is encouraged. Not long after the World Wide Web was invented by computer scientist Tim Berners-Lee, who was then a fellow at the European Organization for Nuclear Research (CERN), the concept of free data sharing was applied to software, leading to the growth of the open-source movement. Open-source pioneers were often seen as "mad scientists" or fringe characters, but in reality, the ideas they were developing and the software they were sharing with millions around the world were the beginning of an innovation mindset and concept that would lead to the Internet as we know it today. Many of them saw the freedom of open source as more than just about price, but about a civic spirit of voluntary cooperation and community collaboration. In many ways, they were advocating for freedom of open co-innovation across all ecosystems.

As the movement took off, corporations saw freely distributed software as a serious threat to their business model, and they tried to crush this idea, demonizing open source as a sickness, theft, and "communism,"[2] but over the years their tone softened quite a bit, and then reversed entirely. In 2016, Ballmer himself, though no longer affiliated with Microsoft by then, stated that he "loved" Microsoft's SQL server, which ran on Linux, and acknowledged that he no longer saw Linux as a threat.[3] Two years later, Microsoft actually purchased GitHub, a leading open-source software repository and platform that makes up the largest open-source community in the world.[4] It only cost the company $7.5 *billion*.[5]

Few of us likely realize how much open source has developed into an integral part of our online activity, the companies we support, and the jobs we perform. It can be found in almost every sector, from education to government, tech to entertainment, financial services to film production.[6] It's become so ubiquitous that we hardly notice it, yet it has fueled an organic explosion in the quality and amount of newly produced software across all domains. Mozilla Firefox, for example, is an open-source software.[7] Wikipedia operates on open source as well.[8] The Android system, which nearly 80 percent of the world's new smartphones run, does too.[9] But to really get a feeling of open source's value and breadth, it's important to note that Linux powers all of the top 500 super computers in the world, along with Facebook, Amazon, eBay, PayPal, Walmart, NASA, and advanced air traffic control.[10] It also powers most of the global financial markets, including the New York Stock Exchange, NASDAQ, the London Stock Exchange, and the Tokyo Stock Exchange.[11] Linux has become the largest, most prevalent open-source software project ever.[12]

None of this would have been possible, however, without the actual developers—a group of over 15,000 individuals from across over 1,400 companies who have been busy contributing to Linux.[13] Some of these companies are typically major competitors, but in a joint effort, they've been collaborating to improve Linux and push open source further into the mainstream—and they're succeeding in their mission. In a 2018 survey, 53 percent of companies who participated stated that they had an open-source program or planned to establish one.[14] Maybe most interestingly, in 2017, research from Harvard Business School found that "open source contributing companies capture up to 100% more productive value from open source than companies that do not contribute back."[15] No matter the intentions of open source's philosophy, its founders, or its suppressors, open source has become big business.

And it's no wonder why. Competition and innovation go hand in hand and lead to better results, but cooperation and co-innovation lead to the *best* results. In open source, we see how innovation blossoms when diverse groups of people work together, sometimes against all odds. All over the world, countries, cities, communities, and companies are creating unprecedented value by uniting and striving toward common objectives. An entire new ecosystem is emerging: large corporations and small startups are connecting in ways they never have before, driving co-innovation that's leading to new offerings across industries. Meanwhile, people from a wide range of businesses, nonprofits, academia, and governments are putting their collective heads together to help improve communities through innovation.

In short, we are living in a world of co-innovation.

No matter the type and size of our organizations, we need to get involved and become part of this greater community. Learning how others operate, and understanding their successes and challenges, will lead to innovations of our own, an increase in shared knowledge, and the generation and execution of better ideas, just like in open source. This means looking outside of the typically narrow view of our immediate competitors to figure out how other businesses, markets, communities, and countries collaborate.

Just as innovation is not the sole domain of one function within a company, it's also not the purview of just one type of business, organization, or industry. It cannot be pigeonholed or tied down. Innovators exist everywhere. They can be seen and called upon more in some areas than others, but given the chance and the right environment, they will emerge no matter what odds they face. In that sense, innovation always takes on a life of its own and is bigger than any organizational, geographical, and political boundaries. Excuse the poeticism, but it's as if innovation wants to be free.

## Come Together

As the saying goes, opposites attract. And that's a good thing for companies today, both big and small. Although they may seem diametrically opposed, the older, somewhat clunky dinosaurs of industry and the younger, dynamic movers and shakers can still learn a lot from one other and accomplish more together. Both are constantly looking for ways to diversify their offerings in an effort to survive and grow. When they pay attention to what the other is doing, they often find that they each have something the other does not, which can normally be broken down into what I'd call youth, or the willingness to take risks, and wealth, of both wisdom and finances.

The benefits of working together are obvious. Startups are known for successfully questioning business realities—from products and services to processes and operations—and as a result come up with new ideas and better ways of solving problems and creating value. Most, however, have very limited capabilities to move their ideas forward, including a lack of experience, an established brand, and time to operate before the investors' cash runs out. Despite being trendy, glamorized, and fawned over, they often lack credibility when attracting customers and partners since they have a limited (and often spotty) track record. Big companies are optimized for scale. They have a tremendous amount of industry knowledge, perspective, and expertise, and they maintain capabilities to take products or services to the public. At the same time, they don't always have insight outside of their industry, a win-together culture, or the flexibility found in most small startups.

The point is that by working together, large and small companies have a better chance to succeed. They can complement one another and provide strengths to make up for their counterparts' weaknesses. For example, a startup may find more exposure working with a Fortune 500, and the Fortune 500 can execute on new ideas far faster with help from the startup. Such collaboration can also lead to subsequent investment or acquisition, helping them turn a hefty profit as well. Since 2010, for example, over 21,800 startup exits have been tracked throughout the world, for a total deal value of around $1.2 trillion.[16]

The impetus to connect and innovate together will often fall on the larger companies—not because startups don't want to, or need to, develop these connections, but because the "big guys" theoretically have more resources to invest in these relationships. That's not to say smaller companies can't make connections the opposite way; if they have an especially novel or interesting idea, reaching out to partner with large organizations may prove fruitful. Companies on both ends of the spectrum need to be realistic with their expectations, have a clear focus, and take a win-win approach.

Unfortunately, most corporate-startup partnerships fail, and there are a variety of reasons why.[17] On the startup side, one of the most common issues is one of trust. Many startups assume that larger companies are only out to steal their intellectual property or their employees. They're worried that they will be taken advantage of, and as a result, they can be suspicious and difficult to work with. More often than not, their worries are unfounded. Transparent goals and proactive discussion about intellectual property can help assuage these concerns, making startups feel more at ease so they can concentrate on creating mutual value, not fretting over poached talent or ideas.

On the corporate side, companies generally act slowly or without a clear focus. Often, there is a strong executive desire to get engaged with startups, but it falls through due to few real objectives, both in goals and metrics. In essence, too many companies create so-called startup petting zoos, in which they run various programs with little measurable impact to the business beyond publicity. Complicated processes, policies, and procedures, coupled with a lack of dedicated ownership and vague communication, also gets in the way of progress, making the experience frustrating for everyone who is involved.

To get beyond these issues, both parties in a corporate-startup relationship should start small and keep it simple, understanding what specific value their engagement can bring to the equation and agreeing on a desired outcome. To succeed long term, these partnerships can't just be about good PR or branding opportunities; they have to be actual working relationships that create joint value and measurable results. Corporations must simplify their processes and ensure engagement and seamless communication with startups from day one; startups must be open and willing to work in a more structured environment than they are potentially used to. Startups and large companies both come out on the losing end when they decline to engage with each other. As long as these partnerships are approached correctly, they will be beneficial all around. Sometimes this means curbing egos and adopting more collaborative mindsets.

If you're part of a startup, make a list of organizations that you might be interested in working with, those that seem aligned in attitude, values, and goals and could potentially help you grow and scale your product. Then reach out and connect with them through as many channels as possible. Don't overlook the largest ones out of fear, as they'll likely end up being the most helpful. If you're a leader in a large organization, and you don't already have a startup engagement program, you should seriously create one. A good first step is to get out of the office and discover what's happening in your local startup community. Attend pitch nights together with your employees so that you all get to know some of the major players in the startup ecosystem. Other great ways to get involved are by connecting your employees with startup mentorship programs or hosting startup meetups at your organization. Engage early and often, but remember, it's best to begin simply. Often a good way to get started is through establishing a relationship with a local innovation accelerator or incubator.

### Innovation Accelerators and Incubators

There are literally thousands of innovation accelerators and incubators around the world, touching almost any industry imaginable. From self-driving cars to biotech, cannabis to the future of digital entertainment, you name it and there's probably an accelerator for it. Innovation accelerators and incubators help startups attract funding, build their capabilities, and scale their ideas to develop profitable products and services. When working at an accelerator or an incubator (I use the two terms interchangeably), startups are given access to resources that help them grow at a faster, though sustainable, rate that would have been unlikely without additional funding or support. Hence, the name "accelerator." What would potentially take a few years, or never make it off the ground to begin with, may only take a few months.

Innovation accelerators can play an important role in helping companies diversify their innovation portfolios and test new products, services, and technologies. As they typically follow a structured process and work in particular areas or industries, they are perfect places for established companies to engage with dozens of startups at a time. They can easily narrow in on those that are involved in projects or initiatives relevant to the companies' business or the business areas that they want to explore. Many organizations open their own innovation accelerators with the sole purpose of working with startups, though not all of them are a success; the majority fail or pivot to another startup engagement approach.

Coca-Cola, for example, began a dedicated program in 2012 to work with startups to create a "repeatable and scalable model for disruptive innovation," but shuttered its doors within five years to, as they stated, focus on "marketing innovation resources primarily around core innovation projects within our beverage portfolio."[18] Up until then, they had helped accelerate an on-demand staffing company called Wonolo and a mobile network for millennials called Weex. Maybe the company realized its focus was off or maybe it just wanted to return to what it does best—create and sell soft drinks—but either way, they decided to work on other ways to engage with startups.

And that type of outcome is okay: starting an accelerator can be a viable tactic for some, but most companies are not necessarily suited for this option, as it may not be core to their business (which was probably one of Coca-Cola's realizations as well). No matter what the industry, a lot of time can be wasted on understanding how to launch an accelerator or how to work with startups to begin with, so a better option for most is to actually partner with an existing accelerator, engaging with their startups and focusing on results rather than infrastructure.

For example, the financial services company Barclays joined with the already existing Techstars accelerator to develop one of their own accelerator programs, which is now spread out in three cities across the world: New York, London, and Tel Aviv.[19] The diamond company the De Beers Group did something similar, partnering with RocketSpace, a Silicon Valley accelerator, innovation consulting company, and co-working campus. Together, they are focusing on programs around technological and digital transformation, including GemFair, a pilot program that uses blockchain technologies for sourcing ethically mined diamonds from small-scale mines.[20]

Whether providing a friendly ear, mentorship and educational opportunities, connections with investors or funding, or deployment of startups' products or services (which is worth gold to them), the larger companies involved end up having a stake in the startups' success, so it's in everyone's best interest to see the projects through to achieve their set goals. Just as the startups receive support, they provide valuable lessons for their corporate partners as well, bringing fresh outside perspective and challenging existing organizational and business dogmas.

No matter the size of your organization, always remember to keep lines of communication open and listen to your partners. Instead of being scared to connect, be excited to connect. Focus on the value that you can both receive and contribute. At the same time, think beyond the immediate short-term gains and embrace the long-term value you can bring to your company, industry, and community. It doesn't matter which side of the aisle you're on, big or small (in fact, don't think of it as an aisle at all!); you need to dispense with the fear of pilfered ideas or talent and focus on the greater picture. And that greater picture is even larger than commerce alone.

## Take Co-Innovation to the Next Level

The emphasis on corporations and startups working together leaves out a crucial element to innovation's freedom: for innovation to succeed in your organization, it's not just other companies that need to be involved—you need to tap into the *entire* ecosystem. That means partnering and co-innovating with customers, suppliers, academia, nonprofits, cities, governments, and more. Not all innovative ideas are born inside the offices of traditional companies (Exhibit A: the Internet). Countries, cities, and municipalities are actively driving new policies to become more innovative on their own and attract new businesses and residents. Academic institutions are expanding research programs toward entrepreneurs. And consumers are starting to feel that their voices are valued unlike ever before, as they have so many ways to connect with companies and make an impact on them.

Engaging with the entire ecosystem leads to a larger pool of opinions and vantage points. As discussed in Chapter 5, diversity creates the best teams. It's no different when looking outside the walls of your office—the more varied the points of view, the better the results. Working with other organizations and groups builds a collective knowledge in an ever-expanding innovation atmosphere. Innovation's not the domain of only one person, one initiative, one company, one industry, or one country. Just like open source, innovation has no borders, no owners—it's everywhere all the time. To that end, if you really want to be innovative you cannot be territorial. You must think creatively and partner with people and groups far and wide, including customers, cities and governments, academia, and nonprofits.

### Customers

Just as employees' ideas, thoughts, and concerns need to play a role in your innovation strategy, so should those of your customers. Why try to guess what they want or need when you can get that information directly from them? When customers are given the opportunity to share their needs and desires in an open setting, you're going to get a lot of good, useable data. By actively asking and listening, you will also solidify your relationship with them and earn their trust. So to be truly successful, go beyond listening and actually try to co-innovate and co-create with your customers. This new relationship could take many different forms and span multiple areas of your business, all the way from marketing to product development.

Crowdsourcing has grown immensely in the digital age, giving consumers the chance to work directly with companies at a scale that would have seemed unimaginable even in the early 2000s. Not only are customers able to have an impact on what companies are offering, but their input works to the advantage of the companies as well, likely saving them loads of cash and years of R&D. Some companies have realized this for a long time and even before the influx of crowdsourcing platforms were taking advantage of their most crucial partners—the ones that actually keep them in business.

Take, for example, the Vermont-based ice cream chain Ben & Jerry's, which is a B-corp, by the way (for a quick refresher on B-corps, return to Chapter 1). Started in 1978 by Ben Cohen and Jerry Greenfield, the company is well-known for their high-quality ingredients and unique flavors, along with their socially and environmentally conscious values. What many cone-licking or pint-gorging fans may not realize is that Ben & Jerry's was a pioneer in adopting crowdsourcing to shape their product portfolio. Some of their most popular flavors began as suggestions from their customers, including the famous Cherry Garcia in 1987, which came in as a recommendation on a postcard.

In 2009, as the company was trying to transition to using all fair-trade ingredients in their products, they launched the Do the World a Flavor campaign, asking customers to come up with their own flavors using only fair-trade ingredients—they received 10,000 submissions.[21] (I'd love to know who gets to make and try all of them.) Not only were they finding out their customers' preferences, but they were partnering with them to innovate toward economic justice and environment sustainability—talk about a win-win-win. Crowdsourcing has taken a center stage since that time, becoming entirely mainstream. Many brands use customer ideas on a regular basis to drive new products or marketing campaigns or pivot their products and service offerings. Customers have become a crucial partner in co-innovation.

### Cities and Governments

Though laissez-faire economists would argue that the best government involvement in business is no government involvement at all, cities and municipalities (and of course their government leaders) play a particularly important role in innovation and are ideal partners. As of 2017, worldwide, three million people per week were moving into urban areas, with 54 percent of the population already living in cities.[22] It has been estimated that by 2050, that number will rise to 66 percent of the global population.[23] Now that's a lot of people, and they're going to need resources, jobs, opportunities, modern infrastructure, amenities, and more. There are also some areas that are favored over others, causing smaller cities and towns to experience brain drain or a net loss of citizens.

In response, a number of cities are increasingly competing to become hotbeds of innovation while improving their citizens' experience. One way they're doing this is by creating innovation hubs, or even by trying to bring in so many companies and organizations that they turn the entire city into an innovation hub itself. Sometimes referred to as innovation communities, labs, or centers, hubs connect startups, government agencies, private enterprises, academics and researchers, customers, and others to explore much more than "business problems." They focus on the overall issues facing communities and individuals today and provide excellent opportunities for co-innovation. City-backed innovation hubs are an example of cooperation between local governments, businesses, and organizations that can lead to benefits for all. Together, they're investing in the creation of stronger communities. These towns become more attractive places to live, providing a larger tax base and greater resources, and businesses work to provide scalable, profitable solutions to problems that can be implemented elsewhere.

The size of the town or city shouldn't really matter either. In fact, my hometown of Carlsbad, California (population 115,000), was one of the earliest cities to embrace this concept with an ambitious innovation strategy and vision.[24] The town set out to improve mobility, sustainability, government services, and civic engagement, while creating a connected economy by partnering with nonprofits, businesses, community groups, and citizens. This strategy gives the city a consistent economic boost from a diverse range of startups, those that either began in town or moved there from other locations. Many big employers also want to be based there because of the town's services, progressive leadership, and vibrant ecosystem. When local governments like the one in Carlsbad take an active role in shaping the innovation agenda for the region, citizens are happier, economic growth takes place, there is an influx of talent, and innovators are given the opportunity to deliver new value.

### Academia

Universities have been playing an increasingly critical role when it comes to co-innovation. Though traditionally known for developing talent and providing cutting-edge academic research, just like every other organization out there, universities are responding to change and evolving as well. They've begun fostering entrepreneurship and driving co-innovation programs with the local ecosystem. They're also attracting students and businesses through major civic initiatives and the development of on-campus innovation hubs, as seen with schools like Georgia Institute of Technology.

The school's hub—the Enterprise Innovation Institute—focuses on networking opportunities and shared knowledge between academic, entrepreneurial, industrial, VC, and public sectors, expanding their local, regional, and global outreach.[25] Part of the impetus comes from Georgia's plans to help transform the surrounding region from a mainly agricultural economy to one that is more innovation-driven.[26] The school's priorities connect with the region's, and they learn from a wide-ranging set of resources, all in the hopes of helping businesses "increase your bottom line, improve competitiveness, and positively impact the economy."[27] They continue to do so through experts in their fields (faculty and students), renowned research, and state-of-the art facilities.

Companies have started taking notice of the Enterprise Innovation Institute's success and are clamoring to work with the hub. Home Depot, for example, established the Home Depot Innovation Center at Georgia Tech, a collaborative space used to recruit top talent and explore how technologies—like 3D printing, virtual and augmented reality, and wearable devices—might advance retail, supply chain solutions, and other related issues. Georgia Tech also hosts innovation and development centers for Anthem, AT&T, Boeing, Chick-fil-A, Delta, Dover, Emerson, Georgia Pacific, Keysight Technologies, Honeywell, NCR, Siemens, Southern Company, Stanley Black & Decker, and more.[28] Since the school opened the innovation hub, it has supported the launch of hundreds of startups, which have raised over $1.5 billion in combined investments.[29]

Even simple initiatives like developing internship programs with universities can help lead to innovation breakthroughs. For example, every year, the Cisco International Internship Program brings together exceptional students from leading universities all over the world to help solve real-life problems and gain hands-on technical experience. Unlike short-term, three-month internships, these students spend a full "gap year" working at Cisco. They learn how to use the latest, greatest technologies the company has to offer and have the time and opportunity to make a real impact in their positions. They also get to meet and befriend other international students, broaden their horizons, and return to their colleges with truly valuable experience and practical skills. (They also have a great time.) Many of them end up getting hired by Cisco or one of their partners later on. In return, Cisco gets a fresh perspective from interns who bring new ideas and challenge the company with fresh thinking and approaches.

Look to broaden your organization's relationship with universities, instead of considering them a mere recruiting ground or pipeline for talent. The tighter your connections, the better, so get involved any way you can. Working with colleges presents an ideal opportunity for your employees to get engaged and give back to the community, while helping your business innovate from the outside in, and then back out into the ecosystem again.

### Nonprofits

Inviting nonprofits into the innovation process is just as important as working with customers, cities, and academia. And it's not just because some nonprofits focus on ideas that create warm fuzzy feelings. They provide a perspective unlike any other, because they are the organizations most tapped into the pressing problems that need to be addressed today, both locally and internationally. Many innovation accelerators and hubs are actually nonprofits as well, including Houston's Station Houston and Chicago's 1871 startup hub.[30]

Chicago's 1871 provides educational opportunities, connections with startups, and resources to build businesses in the Chicago area, while Station Houston focuses on funding opportunities to invest in programs that support local entrepreneurs and the energy, transportation, and industrial sectors. On a global level, nonprofits like the United Nation's World Food Programs Innovation Accelerator are working to help solve issues with hunger and food scarcity around the world. These ambitious goals can only be successful through co-innovation, with groups, institutions, and individuals connecting across the ecosystem. It's really innovation's time to shine.

Consider the Global Coalition to End Wildlife Trafficking Online. In 2018, the World Wildlife Fund, TRAFFIC (a wildlife monitoring organization), and the International Fund for Animal Welfare joined together to partner with a number of social media, tech, and e-commerce companies to eradicate a growing scourge of illegal, black market, online wildlife traffickers. According to Crawford Allan, the senior director of wildlife crime at the World Wildlife Fund and TRAFFIC, "Criminal groups and illegal traders are exploiting the technology to operate anonymously online with less chance of detection and to reach a wider market than ever before."[31] They're less likely to get caught, and they have more customers than ever. For example, every year, more than 20,000 African elephants are illegally killed for their tusks.[32]

Companies who have joined the coalition include well-known American corporations Google, Etsy, eBay, Facebook, and Microsoft, along with Asian firms such as Wen Wan Tian Xia, Zhongyikupai, and Zhuanzhuan. By collaborating, the group hopes to reduce wildlife trafficking across online platforms by 80 percent come 2020.[33] Not only are the companies creating algorithms to catch keywords and flag posts selling these illegal wares, but they're also providing resources for manual reviews, with the WWF training companies' teams on how to evaluate individual posts. The idea is for all of these organizations to share what they learn about emerging trends on their own sites and platforms and the best practices they develop to prevent loopholes for the traffickers, who often jump from one platform to another once they've gotten the boot.

This crowdsourcing approach illustrates the power and possibilities when organizations work together in a whole ecosystem, not just in disconnected compartments. They're from all over the world, swapping their unique processes with a shared goal in mind. Together, they'll be able to make a difference that they'd be unlikely to make separately, all in the name of doing something good for the planet. Sure, they receive some good PR, but this is a true collective display of compassion, powered through innovation. When companies take such bold approaches, they can enact change.

### Innovation for All

There are plenty of opportunities to partner with others and exchange valuable knowledge and ideas. These relationships will help you achieve your set strategy and continue to grow, but they'll also make your community, locally or globally, a better place. Companies, nonprofits, cities, and other organizations willing to share knowledge and embrace the concept of building the innovation ecosystem will certainly see their impact metrics improve, but they'll also be working toward a greater good. The bigger the innovation ecosystem, the more all of the related organizations and institutions reap the benefits of co-innovation.

The groups involved find new ideas, partnerships, and opportunities that would likely have been unavailable otherwise. In learning about what's going on in other industries, markets, and spaces, a larger knowledge base develops. Yes, competition still exists, and you won't find competitors singing "Kumbaya" in a circle around the water cooler or the kombucha tap, but when this knowledge is passed back and forth and shared, innovation thrives and so does society.

In joining an ecosystem and engaging others, innovators are given free range. They go beyond our teams, companies, and industries and begin having even larger impacts. Don't get me wrong—you likely came to this book for advice on improving *your* company's bottom line, not someone else's, but this type of co-innovation has the potential to do both, while also making a positive change in the world. And I hope that's something we can all get behind.

## Case Study: IKEA

Most seventeen-year-olds don't start companies that turn into multibillion-dollar operations—even Mark Zuckerberg didn't launch Facebook until he was nineteen.[34] But in 1943, Ingvar Kamprad, likely still with pimples on his face, set out on his first major business venture. Though he'd been selling an array of goods for years in his small hometown in Sweden—starting with matches at age five, then moving up to pencils and seeds,[35] fish and Christmas cards[36]—the young entrepreneur began hocking wallets, stockings, and pens under the brand name IKEA that year.[37] Furniture, however, would turn out to be his goldmine, which he began selling in 1948.[38] Good fortune followed—a lot of it—and by the time Kamprad passed away at age 91 in 2018, he left behind an incredible legacy and a company with nearly $46 billion in annual revenue.[39]

Since pioneering the concept of mega retail, the empire that Kamprad founded continues to grow, with 492 stores across 49 countries.[40] IKEA no longer focuses only on sleek, easy-to-assemble furniture either—most people don't realize that the company is actually the world's sixth largest food chain,[41] grossing a whopping $1.8 billion in food sales in 2017 (that's a lot of Swedish meatballs).[42] Though it can be hard for multinationals of this size to maintain innovation efforts, IKEA has proven that it's not just possible, but profitable. To do so, they consistently experiment with new ideas and take an open, co-innovation approach to many of their products across a variety of channels, working directly with customers to understand their needs and develop solutions to the problems they face.

The company focuses on three areas of "co-creation": customers' life at home, ideas and prototypes, and voting and feedback.[43] By conducting surveys and polls, asking for photos, and requesting customer workarounds for product issues, IKEA's teams find out what customers are looking for and what they do to improve on IKEA's current offerings. Whether considering comfort in small spaces, storage, engineered wood, the effects of scent in the home, cables cluttering the floor, or cooking, eating, and serving food, they try to cover every aspect of modern-day living. They publish all of their findings back to their consumers, creating transparency and building trust. From there, they develop prototypes, starting with 3D renders or models, and then they share

(*continued*)

## Case Study: IKEA (*continued*)

these with the public, asking customers to vote on which ones they like best. It's all part of their "democratic design," which is focused on "low price, quality, sustainability, form, and function."[44] But customers can get even more involved.

IKEA also has a dedicated online platform, Co-Create IKEA, where customers have the chance to develop and test new products. Torbjörn Lööf, one of the key IKEA group executives, said it's "a bit like open-source development within IT."[45] The company even created "Delaktif," with famed British designer Tom Dixon, an "open-source" sofa that allows any third party to create additional components or products that connect with, or can be used together with, the sofa itself. IKEA is actually open-sourcing furniture! IKEA also develops opportunities for startups, connections with innovation hubs, and collaborations with universities. In the meantime, they've been working with partners to source all of their wood from sustainable sources by 2020 and trying to reach a level of 100 percent renewable energy.[46]

Through all these efforts, IKEA is creating a vibrant ecosystem, working with innovators across the world to co-innovate, co-work, and crowdsource, incorporating a diversity of opinions and ideas that may otherwise be overlooked. These consistent steps to grow their business and provide positive solutions means they're creating and capturing more value, not just for the company alone, but for its customers as well. Taking cues from the open-source philosophy, they're helping innovation develop far beyond their company walls, making sure it remains free.

## Summary: The Freedom of the Ecosystem

To develop successful innovation strategy, we need to open our minds, and eyes, to the innovations that are taking place around us every day. We must of course remain focused on our goals and know what's happening within our teams, down the hall, and in our industries, but we also need to look beyond these typical environments, working together across organizations and with communities near and far. The most practical and productive way to do this is to partner with other public and private organizations, sharing knowledge, ideas, and resources to meet customer demands and solve pressing problems.

Major corporations and small startups each have their own unique attributes, but together, they can work to each other's strengths, making up for weaknesses through programs like innovation accelerators. Customers are emerging as co-innovators, and cities can co-innovate with businesses and citizens to make their services and communities better. When academia and nonprofits join in the mix, innovation can help pull all sorts of organizations together to work toward a common social, economic, or environmental goal.

When all of these groups combine, they build a collective knowledge and create an incredible community, one that must be supported and embraced that can truly help make this world a better place. No matter how organizations decide to engage with others, someone still needs to make sure the hard work gets done. Innovation belongs to everyone and must be supported as such, but, as we'll see in the following chapter, strategy still needs to be orchestrated and someone, or some group, must take the lead.

### Principle

Opportunities rarely occur within our four walls alone—as the world becomes more connected, embracing the ecosystem is essential to success.

### Action

- Discover and engage with the local startup community
- Partner with companies, large and small, to create new value.
- Look at ways to co-innovate with customers.
- Work with cities, academia, and nonprofits to solve problems that are bigger than one industry's alone.

### Obstacles

There's a tendency to remain insular out of ego and fear, which causes organizations to miss out on the major benefits they would otherwise receive when working with the entire ecosystem.

### Outcome

A win-win relationship with others that opens opportunities and creates new measurable value for everyone involved.

## Notes

1. Thomas C. Greene, "Ballmer: 'Linux Is a Cancer,'" *Register*, June 2, 2001, https://www.theregister.co.uk/2001/06/02/ballmer_linux_is_a_cancer/.
2. Graham Lea, "MS' Ballmer: Linux Is Communism," *Register*, July 31, 2000, https://www.theregister.co.uk/2000/07/31/ms_ballmer_linux_is_communism/.
3. Liam Tung, "Ballmer: I May Have Called Linux a Cancer but Now I Love It," *ZDNet*, March 11, 2016, https://www.zdnet.com/article/ballmer-i-may-have-called-linux-a-cancer-but-now-i-love-it/.
4. Tom Warren, "Microsoft Completes GitHub Acquisition," *Verge*, October 26, 2018, https://www.theverge.com/2018/10/26/17954714/microsoft-github-deal-acquisition-complete.
5. Ibid.
6. Linux Foundation, "About the Linux Foundation," 2019, https://www.linuxfoundation.org/about/.
7. JAX Editorial Team, "Know Your History—Open Source's Software Freedom Movement," *JaxEnter*, September 26, 2018, https://jaxenter.com/know-your-history-open-source-149919.html.
8. Klint Finley, "Why 2018 was a Breakout Year for Open Source Deals," *Wired*, December 23, 2018, https://www.wired.com/story/why-2018-breakout-year-open-source-deals/.
9. Linux Foundation, "About the Linux Foundation."
10. Joey Sneddon, "25 Awesome Things Powered By Linux," *omg! ubuntu!*, May 22, 2019, https://www.omgubuntu.co.uk/2016/08/25-awesome-unexpected-things-powered-linux.
11. Linux Foundation, "About the Linux Foundation."

12. Ibid.

13. Jonathan Corbet and Greg Kroah-Hartman, "2017 Linux Kernel Development Report," Linux Foundation, 2017, https://www.linuxfoundation.org/2017-linux-kernel-report-landing-page/.

14. https://www.linuxfoundation.org/uncategorized/2018/08/corporate-open-source-programs-are-on-the-rise-as-shared-software-development-becomes-mainstream-for-businesses/

15. https://papers.ssrn.com/sol3/papers.cfm?abstract_id=3091831.

16. Serena Orizi, "Startup M&A Worldwide: a $1.2 Trillion Market Led by US and Europe," *Mind the Bridge*, September 12, 2018, https://mindthebridge.com/startup-ma-worldwide/.

17. Christian Vogt, "Three Reasons Why Corporate-Startup Partnerships Fail," *Medium*, November 4, 2018, https://medium.com/premainstream/three-reasons-why-corporate-startup-partnerships-fail-19bd647aa458.

18. Natalie Mortimer, "Coca-Cola Is Saying Goodbye to its Start-up Incubator," *Drum*, January 5, 2017, https://www.thedrum.com/news/2017/01/05/coca-cola-saying-goodbye-its-start-up-incubator.

19. Barclays, "Barclays Accelerator," *Barclaysaccelerator.com,* 2019, https://www.barclaysaccelerator.com/#/.

20. RocketSpace, "De Beers Group's GemFiar and Tracer Move into RocketSpace Campus in London," *Globe Newswire*, December 20, 2018, https://www.globenewswire.com/news-release/2018/12/20/1670038/0/en/De-Beers-Group-s-Gem-Fair-and-Tracr-move-into-RocketSpace-campus-in-London.html.

21. http://smbp.uwaterloo.ca/2016/02/ben-jerrys-do-the-world-a-flavor-generates-new-flavor-ideas/.

22. Alice Charles, "Cities Need to innovate to survive. Here Are Four Ways They Can Do It," *World Economic Forum*, February

10, 2017, https://www.weforum.org/agenda/2017/02/cities-must-tirelessly-innovative-to-respond-to-their-challenges/.

23. Ibid.

24. Steve Puterski, "Carlsbad Hires First Chief Innovation Officer," *Coast News*, November 28, 2018, https://www.thecoastnews.com/carlsbad-hires-first-chief-innovation-officer/.

25. Georgia Tech, Enterprise Innovation Institute, "About Us," *GaTech.edu*, 2019. https://innovate.gatech.edu/about-us/.

26. Jan Youtie and Philip Shapira, "Building an Innovation Hub: A Case Study of Transformation of University Roles in regional technological and economic development," *Research Policy*, September 2008, https://www.researchgate.net/publication/222700829_Building_an_innovation_hub_A_case_study_of_the_transformation_of_university_roles_in_regional_technological_and_economic_development.

27. Georgia Tech, Enterprise Innovation Institute, "About Us."

28. Georgia Tech, "Corporate Innovation Centers and Partners," *gatech.edu*, 2019. https://www.gatech.edu/innovation-ecosystem/innovation-centers.

29. Georgia Tech, Venture Lab, "About Us," *venturelab.gatech.edu*, 2019, https://venturelab.gatech.edu/about-us/.

30. Station Houston, https://www.bizjournals.com/houston/news/2019/01/08/station-houston-restructures-into-a-non-profit.html; Chicago's 1871: https://1871.com/about-cec/.

31. Rachael Bale, "Google, Facebook, and Other Tech Giants Unite to Fight Wildlife Crime Online," *National Geographic*, March 7, 2018, https://news.nationalgeographic.com/2018/03/wildlife-watch-tech-companies-online-wildlife-crime-coalition/.

32. Elizabeth Davis, "Leading Tech Companies Unite to Stop Online Wildlife Traffickers," *WorldWildLife.org*, March 7.

2018, https://www.worldwildlife.org/press-releases/leading-tech-companies-unite-to-stop-online-wildlife-traffickers.

33. Ibid.

34. Tom Huddleston Jr., "Here's How 19-year-old Mark Zuckerberg Described 'The Facebook' in His First TV Interview," *CNBC: Make It*, April 17, 2018, https://www.cnbc.com/2018/04/16/how-mark-zuckerberg-described-the-facebook-in-his-first-tv-interview.html.

35. Bloomberg, "Ikea Founder Ingvar Kamprad Dies at 91," *Fortune.com*, January 28, 2018, https://fortune.com/2018/01/28/ingvar-kamprad-ikea-founder-dies/.

36. Forbes, "2015 Billionaires Net Worth: #497 Ingvar Kamprad & family," *Forbes.com*, 2018, https://www.forbes.com/profile/ingvar-kamprad/#52bfad7317f4.

37. Bloomberg, "Ikea Founder."

38. Ibid.

39. Forbes, *Forbes.com*, 2018.

40. Bloomberg, "Ikea Founder."

41. Mark Wilson, "Ikea Is Now the World's 6th Largest Food Chain, and It's Testing Delivery to Your Door," *Fast Company*, June 20, 2019, https://www.fastcompany.com/90365173/ikea-is-now-the-worlds-6th-largest-food-chain-and-its-launching-delivery.

42. IKEA, "Ingka Holding BC and Its Controlled Entities: Yearly Summary FY17," *Ikea.com,* 2017, https://www.ikea.com/ms/da_DK/pdf/yearly_summary/ikea-group-yearly-summery-fy17.pdf.

43. IKEA, "How We Co-create," *Ikeacocreation.com*, 2019, https://ikeacocreation.com/how-we-co-create/.

44. Ibid.

45. Ting, "IKEA: Crowdsourcing Ideas to Co-create a Better Everyday life," *Harvard Business Review: Digital Innovation and Transformation, MBA Student Perspectives*, March 25, 2018, https://digital.hbs.edu/platform-digit/submission/ikea-crowdsourcing-ideas-to-co-create-a-better-everyday-life/.

46. IKEA, "We're Going All-in for a More Sustainable Future," *IKEA: People and Planet*, 2019, https://www.ikea.com/ms/en_US/this-is-ikea/people-and-planet/index.html.

# Chapter 7

## Outcomes Must Be Orchestrated

It's almost hard to imagine, but there was a time, not long ago, that information technology was seen as a peripheral function. You probably thought of IT as the department you called if your computer screen was frozen, while praying that the document that you'd been working on for the entire day had been properly saved and could be recovered. Aside from that, and the occasional printer jam or network outage, this may have been your only interaction with IT. In just a few decades, information technology has become core to nearly all business, as every organization is becoming digital to one extent or another. Business survival and growth is impossible without technology, so IT is now essential, and chief information officers, a job that was once seen by many as odd or unnecessary, are commonplace. If the rise of chief information officers is any barometer, then chief *innovation* officers' time has come. Innovation is *bigger* than any information technology alone; part science, part art, it's about people, culture, skills, processes, and a new era of work.

The concept of the chief innovation officer has only recently emerged, and is in many ways still emerging. In fact, it's so fresh that people have yet to agree on a simple acronym to describe the position—chief information officers, established earlier, have claimed CIO for their own, and CINO just hasn't caught on, though not for a lack of trying. The job scope is not uniform either, so there are many job descriptions and titles in the mix, like "vice president of innovation," "vice president of growth," "chief technology innovation officer," or "chief digitization officer." Just as many companies have little clarity when it comes to innovation, they seem to be missing clarity when it comes to this role as well.

Maybe that's because chief innovation officers somewhat resemble "chief everything officers," taking on the immense task of transforming the entire culture of an organization. Chief innovation officers don't seem to last long, though, either a result of poor performance, a lack of clear expectations, or no commitment to innovation itself by the company. That's why so many chief innovation officers end up with the word "former" in their title. Sometimes companies just don't really know why they need them or how to leverage them. Tim Cook, the well-known CEO of Apple, has even apparently said that "as soon as a company has a Chief Innovation Officer you know that a company has a problem."[1] I beg to differ, and I think many companies are missing the point.

Chief innovation officers are dedicated executive-level leaders, typically reporting to the CEO, who drive innovation across all levels of the organization. Every organization is unique, so each one may define the role in a unique way, but in basic terms, it's the chief innovation officer's job to create an innovation-friendly environment. They help develop and drive strategy, identify and capture opportunities, support and encourage skills, and evangelize for innovation companywide, often by finding shelter for promising projects. Innovation officers are here to push innovation forward when it starts to lag behind—a dedicated person to help direct all things innovation.

"But wait!" you might say. "Doesn't innovation belong to everyone? Didn't I just read that a mere few pages ago in this very book, Alex?" True, it most certainly does belong to everyone. As chief innovation officers become more prevalent, they aren't taking innovation away from anyone else—just as in reality no team in particular can "own" innovation, nor can chief innovation officers. When I think of the rise of chief innovation offices, I think of a Milton Friedman quote: "When everybody owns something, nobody owns it, and nobody has a direct interest in maintaining or improving its condition."[2] Simply said, there must be a place in your organization for an individual or group who can work cross-functionally to enable innovation. They will not only hold others accountable, but also be accountable themselves, as they are measured on the outcomes of innovation, in whatever way the company defines them.

Such support for innovation doesn't only have to come from a chief innovation officer; it can also be found in innovation governance and through innovation teams, all of which act together to put it front and center and help keep it on track. Innovation requires a process to gain credibility and occur in logical steps (even if they seem illogical to the rest of the business). Organizations therefore need dedicated employees, not just the middle managers and leaders discussed in Chapter 2, to help lead that vision and strategy. Innovation often requires a full-on cultural change, but that can't happen if we don't first understand why innovation so often fails to take root in our organizations, and how to orchestrate its success, across all levels. We must ensure that it grows, instead of letting it become another forgotten initiative or an unkept marketing campaign promise.

## Don't Let Innovation Get Lost

In a perfect world, innovation would be so seamlessly intertwined with an organization, it would be unnoticeable, and the need for dedicated executives, cross-company governance, and teams would cease to exist. Until then, however, all three are absolutely vital for your organization to be successful. Otherwise, when "innovation transformation initiatives" are created, they remain just that: initiatives. They can be set aside, thrown out, defunded, forgotten, lost, or replaced with others. Sadly, more often than not, these shiny initiatives start with fanfare but then are quietly dropped and forgotten. Scott Kirsner, my colleague introduced in Chapter 3, said it best in a piece for *Harvard Business Review*: "When a CEO announces a major initiative to foster innovation, mark your calendar. Three years later, many of these ambitious ventures will have quietly expired without an obituary."[3] Nothing truer on the topic may have ever been stated.

Everyone wants a piece of innovation these days. It's seen as cool, creative, and newsworthy; it's what all the startups aim for and what the corporations hope to attain (as if innovation could be owned). And companies do so much to *try* to be innovative. They work with startups, launch accelerators, create Silicon Valley outposts, drive technology scouting programs, move to open floor plans with ambient mood lighting, and hire personal chiefs who create organic meals from local, sustainable ingredients. But that doesn't necessarily mean they succeed.

Whether talking about culture, digitization, or a transition to new economic and business realities, there's been an increase in senior executives being very vocal about the critical role innovation plays, regularly stating how committed they are to its success. When they speak about it, everyone in the organization seems to hear them, yet innovation gains little traction. In the words of Scott Emmons, the former head of the Neiman Marcus innovation lab, "processes are broken, execution is too slow, politics stalls decision-making and resources are too scarce."[4]

For many, getting things done is not necessarily "fun." It's not always as exciting as launching an innovation competition or cutting a ribbon for a bigger innovation lab. The full spectrum of innovation requires a lot of back-office work, which could be perceived by many as "boring," "noncreative," or, worse, "not important." In reality, though, this back-office work—strategy, planning, operations, finance, product management—is what sets successful innovation apart from overhyped initiatives that lead to failure. Successful innovation requires a perfect balance of creativity and discipline.

For innovation to survive and prosper, organizations need to focus on the milestones that will lead to true transformation, the type of change that translates into innovation as a normal way of doing business. Unfortunately, this rarely happens, because often no one is there to drive alignment and ensure that the hard work gets done. If the leadership team is not aligned and there's no group or person focused on developing innovation strategy and executing on it, then true change will never be within reach.

Invoking the promise of innovation without the ability to make good on it can only lead to one outcome: failure. Besides demotivating the troops, failure is costly, and as many leaders have discovered before, it's quite hard to recover from initiatives that have gone off the rails. When an organization is truly innovative, innovation is seen and felt everywhere—it's contagious, like laughter or the feeling of happiness that rubs off from a group of other happy people. But this type of built-in innovation, so regular that it's nearly untraceable, doesn't just appear one day. It needs a helping hand.

## Hire a Chief Innovation Officer

With the rise of chief innovation officers, or whatever you'd like to call them, more companies are opening up to incorporating such a position into their operations in a serious way. In fact, the word "company" is too narrow a scope. Chief innovation officers are being hired throughout various organizations and even by cities, counties, and states. Starting with Brian Sivak in 2011, who was appointed as Maryland's chief innovation officer, and then Jay Nath in 2012, who was appointed director of innovation for the City and County of San Francisco, chief innovation officers have been popping up in city governments all over the US, with 25 as of 2018.[5] They fill a similar role in these positions as they would at any organization, setting the vision and strategy and executing on innovation initiatives.

Some of them focus on tech, but more often than not, they're looking at the whole ecosystem within the given city, county, or state, for economic opportunities, quality of life issues, and generally ways to improve and grow. For example, Sacramento's chief innovation officer, Louis Stewart, has taken a holistic view of the job, driving tech *and* other economic and education programs, with a focus on underserved neighborhoods, while Los Angeles created a specific Office of Extraordinary Innovation in 2015, hiring Dr. Joshua L. Schank to push more efforts toward mobility in the perennially gridlocked city.[6]

As part of Carlsbad's innovation efforts, mentioned in the previous chapter, it was the first city in San Diego County to create the position of chief innovation officer. Last year the position was filled with a veteran local government leader, David Graham, who left his post at the City of San Diego as the Deputy Chief Operating Officer for Smart & Sustainable Communities to take the position. He reports directly to the city manager but works with all of the city's departments to future-proof transit services and improve public safety, among many other things. Having someone in this role who understands technology is great, and it's even more important to have leaders who know how to think differently, keep up with the times, and find modern solutions to problems all local governments face. Such a chief innovation officer has long been necessary in many communities and is now being realized in Carlsbad and other cities.

Of course, chief innovation officers aren't a cure-all, and they come with their own potential issues. Aside from the fact that there's still a great deal of inconsistency in how their role is defined (or turned into an acronym), they have a lot of trouble being accepted across organizations. That's in part because the position is still fairly new, but it's also because they're dealing with the typical office issues: egos, fear, lack of empowerment and focus, disengagement, and an inability to get everyone to see eye to eye across the entire organization (which can of course be thousands and thousands of people).

Though they have a broad, cross-functional role, they can still become siloed. This happens since they are often in charge of innovation labs or company accelerators, causing them to be less involved with the overall organization and focusing instead only on their own projects, rather than focusing on freeing innovation and making it relevant to all. Chief innovation officers' jobs are far from easy; whoever is in the position needs to be prepared to face plenty of the obstacles, including pushback from other members of the organization who want to stick to the old norms or expect ambiguous overnight innovation miracles. If chief innovation officers succeed in spreading innovation and creating results, then everyone throughout the organization receives the credit and praise; if they fail to do so, then they take all the blame.

In hiring chief innovation officers, it's critical to find the right fit. Of course, they must have vision and good ideas, but without the intent or capability to execute, they're pretty much worthless, to say the least, and are likely to be a liability to your organization. They need to be so much more than so-called "thought leaders" or "industry visionaries" with a penchant for hearing themselves talk. Unfortunately, some arrive in their new position with a major ego in tow and the belief that the job is nothing more than charm, executive presence, and a nice title and paycheck. This happens more often than might be expected: companies make the mistake of bringing in people who don't end up driving anything, except their sports car to the office. Not all thought leaders are like this of course, but those that are egocentric, the kind that use "I" more than "we," will not do your organization any good. Innovation officers need to be the dealmakers, operational gurus, and champions of innovation, truly believing in a "win together" innovation mindset and advocating for it throughout the organization. In fact, every function needs these type of change agents, no matter what they're called. Thankfully, these leaders are growing in number and people everywhere are truly starting to take notice.

Still, there's a long way to go for chief innovation officers—as mentioned, the job survival rate is actually quite small—not because they're failing, but because a misconception of what innovation is, or isn't, persists. If the need for innovation is not clear and goals are not defined, as they so often aren't, then chief innovation officers will run into issues when trying to show their worth and put their plans into action. Unlike many other leaders, they also tend to be forward-looking and more focused on tomorrow than today, so when results aren't immediate in the short-term, their peers can quickly lose attention or fail to see the officers' value. It has even been argued that innovation officers are altogether unnecessary, as innovation should be organization-wide, and not be dependent on one person alone, but obviously those making this argument don't understand the realities of driving innovation. Until they do, there's luckily an additional way to ensure that innovation outcomes are orchestrated—through the help of governance processes.

## Put Governance Processes into Action

Yes, "governance" sounds very bureaucratic, and when I hear the word, I often think, as I'm sure most other people do, "Here comes death by PowerPoint." But governance is actually very simple: it's a mutual agreement to reach set goals together and hold one another accountable. By collectively executing strategy, outcomes are more likely to be supported and reached. The smaller your organization, the easier this process will be. For any larger, distributed organization, ensuring that everyone is on the same page and is marching toward a common goal requires some major effort. An innovation governance process ensures that this effort is realized. Don't get me wrong, I don't want my innovation project to be run by a tribal council, yet I realize that in any organization there needs to be a happy medium between autonomy and structure that offers value to everyone. So, the ideal innovation governance process must be transparent, open, and inclusive—and incredibly flexible.

At a bare minimum, innovation governance processes should help organizations come to an agreement on their key innovation priorities, metrics, and their team members' particular duties and roles, hopefully avoiding a duplication of work and minimizing failure, as well as expense reports. At a more advanced level, governance will allow a transparent and pragmatic (rather than political) distribution of the appropriate funding toward meaningful programs that are related to clear organizational goals, not executive pet projects. This transparency will lead to healthy discussions, both among executives and with employees as a whole, about innovation, required investments, and the value that is created.

This process is especially important in larger companies, particularly those that are introducing innovation initiatives for the first time or those recovering from previously failed attempts. Whenever there's a new initiative or venture, there needs to be a decision made on how much will be invested in that area—that is if the initiative is worth the investment to begin with. Thanks to innovation governance, conscious decisions will be made over which initiatives will be supported and which aren't worth the investment. If you've been running multiple innovation programs, you may find that, on reexamination, some need to actually be de-invested.

While many argue that innovation needs a limitless credit line for some promise of unknown discoveries, funding formulas for innovation should be no different than those for sales, marketing, product development, or any other department. They must be based on opportunity, the return on investment, and your risk tolerance. Innovation needs sustainable investment to develop, but it's essential that there is a connection between investment and the resulting value, thus holding everyone in the organization accountable for the outcomes.

Keep in mind that this governance process takes place in the context of survival, efficiency, aspiration, or growth (as outlined in Chapter 2). When allocating resources, you have to consider all these factors and balance immediate needs with future growth. Unless you have governance, the future will rarely get prioritized. And that's no way to instill innovation within your organization. In fact, according to a *Harvard Business Review* study of 5,000 board members worldwide, companies who have a greater focus on the long term, as compared to achieving short-term goals, are more likely to "have boards that prioritize innovation."[7]

As with any type of forward-looking approach, it comes down to risk versus reward and the availability of resources. You need to decide what new innovations are worth supporting and how, given all of the information you have today, with an eye toward tomorrow. Without transparent governance and representation from all company functions, you won't know what to prioritize, strategy will get lost, and teams will end up working against one another, scrapping for resources while their so-called leaders are fighting one another for a more impressive-sounding innovation title. While this situation sadly can be quite normal in a large company, it doesn't have to be. Innovation governance helps prevent these problems, while enabling innovation to keep moving forward. It deals with conflicts of interest and ensures execution toward long-term goals through a clear and transparent approach across all functions. Innovation governance is a conscious step toward creating a better future—or actually any future at all—and is critical to supporting the third aspect of orchestrating innovation outcomes: innovation teams.

## Build Innovation Teams

Think of the best project managers or facilitators you ever worked with. They most likely didn't constantly tell you what to do or micromanage your every move. Instead, they were there to assist in bridging the gap between your set plans and the execution of those plans. Their goal was to stay focused, resolve issues, and move projects forward toward goals. It's almost like in a hostage negotiator situation: they're not there for themselves, they're there to free the hostage. Could you imagine negotiators telling kidnappers what *they* wanted? No, they're only there to facilitate the process, humbly and almost invisibly. Innovation teams often act in the same way—they're trying to free innovation. After all, the concept is what created all organizations to begin with, but it often gets kidnapped by politics and stagnation. Innovation teams help enable an organization and its employees and remove roadblocks by gently facilitating the innovation process.

To reach this goal, there is no one "right" way to structure an innovation team. Each model depends on your organization's particular circumstances, and it comes down to what works best with your organizational DNA. Just like with humans, company DNA has a certain degree of plasticity, and it can change, transform, and reorganize when introduced to a new environment, in this case, one that is fully connected to innovation. Typically, there are three approaches to structuring innovation teams: centralized, decentralized, and a hybrid of the two.

### Centralized

Centralized innovation teams are usually set up in a way so as to be separated from other teams and operations. They're given the "innovation team" designation and are tasked with innovation projects, working on implementing new initiatives, whether the dreaded "billion-dollar moonshot" or the more practical development of new products and services or business models. These teams typically have their own budget that comes directly from the CEO or an executive leadership team. Though they still act as facilitators, they tend to be more insular, which, as I hope you've realized by now, can lead to some major issues.

On the plus side, centralized control means a laser focus and the flexibility and speed to move on new opportunities almost as soon as they arise. On the down side, it's easy for the silo mentality to find its way in, meaning the teams aren't always aligned with what else is happening in the rest of the organization. While in theory they are often mandated in driving innovation for the entire company, they tend to do so only within their team, which means co-innovation falters companywide and those initiatives keep getting lost, never to become actual day-to-day business practices.

Centralized teams work well in areas where silos are necessary—like the military or pharmaceutical companies (as mentioned in Chapter 6)—or in small organizations whose portfolios aren't diversified with multiple business units. In general, small companies lend themselves to centralized teams, since most everyone is more likely to be working in concert together. These teams can also be successful if they find a way to engage with others in the organization and get the rest of the business on board early on. Of course, that's no easy task, and all the speed and flexibility in the world can't ensure that this will happen.

### Decentralized

Decentralized teams are those that are developed throughout the organization, within separate business units or functions. They are typically funded by the specific business and their innovation efforts are normally adjacent to the core business. Like centralized teams, however, speed is one of their strengths. Since they report to the business unit leaders, they act as a subset of that business unit, essentially a team within a team, and they therefore don't need to deal with as much red tape or politics to move forward on projects.

Unfortunately, also like centralized teams, silos can become an issue. If each business unit has a team, the more business units you have, the more competing silos you create. Once teams start competing to become the "most innovative," the focus on innovating together for greater value disappears. Decentralized teams are useful for large organizations that naturally have a diversified portfolio. They can be successful if they find ways to engage with others cross-functionally and co-innovate toward common goals.

### Hybrid

In the hybrid model, one or more teams exist that may work on various innovation projects. For example, one may be focused on venture investing, while another one handles startup initiatives, and still another takes on product development. It sounds a bit like the decentralized model, but in this one, there is also a centralized organizational function that drives alignment and coordination between all other teams for greater yet pragmatic purposes. This is obviously the type of team that I believe is the best, as it works toward real transformation.

Hybrid teams work to accomplish the same overall goals as the rest of the organization. They are not off somewhere "doing innovation," but continuously connecting with the rest of the company to ensure alignment and execution of strategy. Regardless of the legal structure, or the org chart, these teams must exist within the organization as part of the environment, not as a separate entity, consistently connecting everyone. This is where a unified approach comes into play, going all the way back to the leader's ability to help develop a comprehensive strategy, as discussed in Chapter 2. When everyone is on board, including the innovation team, that's when things really start to come together. This hybrid approach works for teams of all sizes as well.

A hybrid team ensures that every function in your organization has a stake in innovation. This means there will be a lot of competing voices that need to find a way to work together. Some may be more vocal than others or think that their particular role should be the main force in pushing innovation strategy. This can cause tension within the groups, so you need to avoid creating different levels of innovators. Therefore, you can't define innovation solely around one function, such as product development, which happens quite often.

Of course, hybrid teams have problems of their own, similar to those in the decentralized and centralized ones. They don't suffer from silos, but just as with any group, office bureaucracy and politics is bound to rear its ugly head. Egos get in the way, especially when it comes to clashing personalities. The innovation team can quickly devolve into a bickering mess of "My idea is bigger than yours." Next thing you know, people are pulling rank or creating political camps and the whole point of the innovation team—gently facilitating innovation—disappears. It's only natural: everyone competes in a corporate environment. But innovation must be democratized within the innovation team, the same as anywhere else throughout the company and beyond.

It doesn't matter what grade, location, or function the team members come from—if they're part of the innovation team, then they have the same goal as everyone else within that hybrid team: orchestrating innovation. By empowering others, they all facilitate innovation and move the organization's strategy and effort forward, which is, of course, their ultimate goal.

## Case Study: Bloomberg Philanthropies

In 1981, Michael R. Bloomberg was let go from Salomon Brothers, a Wall Street investment bank that he had begun working for in 1966, where he started in an entry-level position fresh out of Harvard Business School. He moved his way up through the company throughout the late '60s and the '70s, holding positions in equity trading, sales, and information systems. But when 1981 rolled around and he was back on the job market, he decided to take a leap into entrepreneurship, founding a little startup called Bloomberg LP. Over the years, his namesake firm has developed into a global data, software, finance, and media company, now employing almost 20,000 people in 120 countries.[8] As his company, and wealth, grew, Bloomberg began focusing more on philanthropic efforts. He may be best known for his three-term run as mayor of New York City, from 2002 through 2013, but he may end up being most remembered for Bloomberg Philanthropies, a charitable organization he established in the early 2000s that focuses on arts and culture, education, public health, the environment, and government innovation.

In his 2019 annual letter on philanthropy, Bloomberg stated, "I'm an optimist: I always believe that tomorrow will be better than today. But I'm also a realist, and I know that believing and hoping won't make it so. Doing is what matters."[9] It's this type of focus on executing outcomes that has contributed to Bloomberg Philanthropies becoming one of the largest philanthropic foundations in the US. Whether looking at ways to help solve problems surrounding climate change, the opioid crisis, gun violence, or public education, the foundation doesn't just contribute money, but tries to create actionable solutions. This effort can clearly be seen in its support of innovation in city governments through proactive sponsorship of innovation teams and chief innovation officers. Acting as in-house innovation consultants, these groups join city governments for three-year stints to focus on handling problems that are specific to the given city.[10]

We're not talking small, easy-to-fix issues here. Starting in 2011, these "i-teams" helped reduce the murder rate in New Orleans, decrease homelessness in Atlanta, and stem the tide of gun violence in Memphis, while also working to improve its underprivileged neighborhoods.[11] As Bloomberg stated,

"Successful innovation depends as much on the ability to generate ideas as it does the capacity to execute them—and i-teams help cities do both."[12] Understanding the need for the additional resources in many city and state governments to get beyond bureaucracy, politics, and gridlock, and to actually help citizens throughout communities, Bloomberg Philanthropies has partnered with the organization Living Cities to further move their city-based innovation efforts forward. Using a mix of technology, data, and on-the-ground community building, they aim to make actual impacts on people's lives around the country.

It's not that city governments are inept (at least not all of them) or that their leaders don't care about constituents; the reality of the matter is that without a dedicated focus on innovation, important work just won't get done. If all municipal governments had innovation built in at the core of what they do, there'd be no need for these types of "innovation interventions." But it's not that easy. Budgets aren't unlimited, and local governments aren't necessarily known for their speed. Until they are, co-innovation efforts like those the Bloomberg Philanthropies supply through its "i-team" program will be necessary to orchestrate outcomes around the most pressing local issues today.

## Summary: Orchestrating Invisible Innovation

Without a full-on commitment to innovation at all levels—from executives to middle managers to employees—innovation will be dead on arrival. Even if employees believe in innovation strategy and are excited about their prospects, that doesn't mean they are impervious to the standard office politics or operations—the "business as usual" that can end up pushing innovation aside. This is possible in any organization, large or small, so there needs to be a support system to help orchestrate the actual outcomes. Any innovation effort needs to be given time to blossom, but there still needs to be a group there to push things forward to make sure it doesn't get stalled. Chief innovation officers, governance processes, and innovation teams enable organizations to do just that, ensuring execution and achievement of long-term goals through measurable milestones. Of course, neither innovation officers nor innovation teams own innovation.

The governance process gives executives, as well as the business units and functions, a much-needed push to provide such support, as they are able to see the successes and failures around innovation and can then decide how and where to spend the finite resources within their organization. From there, goals can be further developed and alignment can take place company wide. Resources must be allocated in a way that focuses not just on short-term gains, but on long-term growth. The ability to invest in this long-term growth often comes down to an ability to communicate the concept and value of innovation and innovation strategy, both internally and externally, which is the topic of our final chapter.

### Principle

Innovation requires credibility and execution in logical steps; a group or individual needs to help enable that process, to help others think big and execute in small measurable milestones, with support through governance.

### Action

- Hire a chief innovation officer to develop comprehensive innovation strategy and execute on it forward.
- Leverage transparent governance process to drive alignment and resource allocation.
- Build innovation teams that work in concert with your overall organization.

### Obstacles

A persistent misunderstanding of the function of innovation teams and chief innovation officers, short-term mindsets, and office politics and egos can lead to arguments over finite resources. Silos contribute to a lack of alignment or companywide buy-in, and an all-around lack of support for innovation strategy.

### Outcome

Innovation is embedded in every function of the organization thanks to the chief innovation officer, transparent and inclusive governance processes, and innovation teams that keep execution on track.

## Notes

1. Richard Angus, "The Chief Innovation Officer—A Symptom or a Solution," *Innovation Enterprise*, November 20, 2019, https://channels.theinnovationenterprise.com/articles/the-chief-innovation-officer-a-symptom-or-a-solution.
2. Ben Duronio, "9 Unforgettable Quotes From Milton Friedman," *Business Insider*, July 31, 2012, https://www.businessinsider.com/milton-friedman-quotes-2012–7.
3. Scott Kirsner, "The Stage Where Most Innovation Projects Fail," *Harvard Business Review*, April 11, 2017, https://hbr.org/2017/04/the-stage-where-most-innovation-projects-fail.
4. Scott Emmons, "Why I'm Leaving Neiman Marcus," *Business of Fashion*, January 15, 2019, https://www.businessoffashion.com/articles/opinion/op-ed-why-im-leaving-neiman-marcus.
5. News Staff, "Chief Innovation Officers in State and Local Government (Interactive Map)," *Government Technology*, August 20, 2018, https://www.govtech.com/people/Chief-Innovation-Officers-in-State-and-Local-Government-Interactive-Map.html.
6. Gargi Chakrabarty, "Why Cities Are Hiring Chief Innovation Officers," *Icons of Infrastructure*, 2018, https://iconsofinfrastructure.com/why-cities-are-hiring-chief-innovation-officers/.
7. J. Yo-Jud Cheng and Boris Groysberg, "Innovation Should Be a Top Priority for Boards," *Harvard Business Review*, September 21, 2018, https://hbr.org/2018/09/innovation-should-be-a-top-priority-for-boards-so-why-isnt-it.
8. Bloomberg Philanthropies, "Mike Bloomberg," Bloomberg Philanthropies, 2019, https://www.bloomberg.org/about/mike-bloomberg/.
9. Michael R. Bloomberg, "Annual Letter on Philanthropy," Bloomberg Philanthropies, 2019, https://annualreport.bloomberg.org/annual-letter/.

10. Jeffrey Stinson, "Chief Innovation Officers: Do They Deliver?" *Government Technology*, February 6, 2015, https://www.govtech.com/state/Chief-Innovation-Officers-Do-They-Deliver.html.

11. Ibid.

12. Ibid.

# Chapter 8

## Communicate, Communicate, Communicate

If you've ever gone out for sushi, chances are you've eaten raw salmon. And why not? It's typically on every sushi menu, and you probably consider it a staple of Japanese cuisine, just like tuna. If you were to travel to Japan, you'd find salmon on sushi menus everywhere as well. It might be hard to believe then, but all of this salmon sushi and sashimi is actually the result of a carefully designed Norwegian government-funded sushi initiative—yes, you read that right. If you had gone to Tokyo back before the '80s, you would not have been able to find salmon sushi anywhere. Sure, you could have ordered cooked salmon as part of some delicious dish, but not raw. Most salmon in Japan—having come from the Pacific—was known for its parasites and would have never been consumed uncooked by the Japanese.[1]

It's funny how perceptions change; or maybe it's not so much funny as it is just a matter of effective communications. Enter Norway and their abundant supply of Norwegian salmon, which, by the way, is now the dominant fish used in sushi restaurants around the world.[2] The 1980s found Norway with a real surplus of the fish. The country's government had subsidized their fishing industry for decades, and by the late '80s decided they needed to stop.[3] They didn't know what to do with the vast amounts of salmon piling up, so they looked to the global market for ideas. That's when they struck on pitching their product to a nation that already ate a lot of fish—Japan. But why sushi? Why not just sell it as a regular old fish that consumers would need to cook? Well, economics, my dear friends: the capitalist dollar (or in this case kroner) at work. Fish for sushi could demand a much higher price than for fish that would be baked, grilled, or smoked.

But just to say, "Eat salmon sushi," wasn't an easy sell, particularly to a nation that knows a thing or two about seafood, and happens to be the ultimate authority on sushi. The thought of raw salmon turned most stomachs in Japan, as the people of the country were convinced they'd get sick from the parasites. Norwegian salmon did not have the same problems as the Pacific salmon—it was totally fine to eat raw, and in fact quite good—but try convincing Japanese customers of that. Well, that's exactly what Norway did.

The Norwegian government started by first listening to their targeted customers to figure out why they were so scared of what seemed like a perfectly good sushi and sashimi fish. Norway actually spent millions on extensive market research just to understand the Japanese perception of salmon sushi.[4] Complaints from customers included that the taste, texture, smell, and color were all off. Some even said the head of the fish was the wrong shape.[5] Once they understood these concerns, Norway put a marketing plan into action, pitching their salmon as fresh, safe, and clean, creating commercials that showed the natural wonder of the country's mountains, fjords, and sea, and they even threw in a Viking cartoon for good measure.[6] Norway's not-so-secret government-backed "Project Japan" was off and running. The government eventually convinced one supplier to buy around 5,000 tons of frozen salmon, which wasn't even that much considering the amount Norway had on ice.[7] It was the first inroad into a huge market.

Norwegian salmon also developed its own brand evangelists in Japan, including celebrity chefs like Yutaka Ishinabe, who would endorse the product on the Japanese cooking show *Iron Chef* in the 1990s.[8] Salmon sushi took off in such a major way that Norway actually started having trouble keeping up with the demand.[9] In time, sushi spread around the world, and the salmon came with it as a staple. Today, Norway's seafood industry is stronger than ever, exporting over 8.6 billion NOK (or around $1 billion USD) worth of seafood in January 2019 alone. Not only did the country alter sushi-eating habits around the world, but the return on Norwegian taxpayers' money has been immense, with a huge boost in the country's economic power and the creation of jobs across Norway. If it weren't for the art of asking the right questions, listening, and an effective marketing and communications campaign, none of this would likely have ever happened.

Though I've hinted at this idea throughout the preceding pages, now that the book is nearing its end, I think it's time to make sure I slam home the principle that often separates success from failure and might just rescue your innovation transformation some day: innovation requires you to communicate, communicate, communicate. And then? Communicate some more.

When communication is at its best, so is innovation. For the concept to take hold, you must communicate effectively with multiple audiences, understanding what they care about and how best to connect with them. Internally, the focus is not just on your employees, but also on your fellow leaders and managers, along with your executives and stakeholders. Externally, you're speaking to your customers and partners of course, but you also want to make your voice heard by the rest of your industry, competitors, collaborators, and the general public, as many of them are potential consumers or employees as well.

You have to identify these internal and external stakeholders, figure out what matters most to them, and constantly reach out to them to get their perspectives and listen to their feedback. Besides giving you priceless information about their desires and needs, this communication will also help you build stronger relationships by giving your stakeholders vested interest in the success of your project. You can't just tell them about lofty concepts either; you have to show them the actual value you're delivering, or will deliver, and how it will benefit them. Remember, no one's here for lip service.

It's common sense that people won't buy your products or services if they aren't aware of their benefits, or their mere existence. The same idea applies to your innovation efforts or programs—whether inside or outside your organization, vertically or horizontally, no one is going to care about them if they don't know about them. And if no one cares, then eventually they'll fail or get defunded, whichever comes first, and you can kiss any potential culture of innovation goodbye.

Moreover, strong communication is necessary when developing and executing on strategy. So even though I suggest shouting the gospel of innovation from the top of any nearby mountains (and across any fjords), communication's even more important when it actually comes to the complex, difficult work of rallying the troops and "getting things done." It's also key to every actionable principle in this book: instilling the urgency of constant change; soliciting employee feedback, getting everyone on the same page, and making strategy easy to understand; setting joint goals and explaining metrics to stakeholders; executing in small measurable milestones; building diverse cross-functional teams; listening and talking to ecosystem partners; and then driving outcomes—none of this is happening without clear, concise, consistent, and creative communication.

## Invest in Communications Skills and Capabilities

With the growth of digital communication, our ability to connect with anyone, anywhere, and at any time has become commonplace. We think nothing of sending out an email (293.6 billion are estimated to go out each day[10]), sharing pictures with complete strangers of meals at sushi joints, and communicating digitally with dozens of "friends" whom we've never met in real life. Most of this book was written while collaborating with my editors on the other side of the country through Webex. We've come a long way from the time verbal communication emerged an estimated 1.75 million years ago.[11] You'd think in that time we'd have it all figured out, but of course, we don't. We have all the technology we need at our fingertips to conduct a last-minute meeting from across multiple time zones, but that doesn't guarantee it will be a productive one. As cultural, social, and technological changes continue, honest conversations in which we all speak *and listen* only become more imperative.

Two-way, open communication is essential in our personal and professional lives, but it is persistently lacking. When it comes to the workplace, it almost seems like leaders and employees barely talk among themselves, let alone to one another. Try asking some people in your office about your company's goals, and you'll probably be *un*pleasantly surprised by the answers you receive. According to one survey, a measly 14 percent of employees understand their company's planned strategy.[12] Only 14 percent! Obviously, the other 86 percent aren't getting the message, assuming someone is communicating the strategy with them in the first place.

Another survey found that only 40 percent of workers know their organization's mission statement (let's not get into the fact that, of that 40 percent, more than half of them are not motivated by this mission).[13] What has truly astonished me over the years is that I've found that most people actually don't seem to know how much money their company is making, what products are being sold outside of their department, and who their top customers are. I'd be amazed if the majority of employees of public companies even listen to their quarterly earnings calls.

Research from 2019 found that executives, talent developers, and people managers believe communication skills are more important than collaboration skills or role specific ones, and almost as critical as leadership skills.[14] Still, investment in communications is generally the last priority in many innovation teams or programs. Leaders pour money into hardware, software, and engineering capabilities, basically anything else but communications. The irony is undeniable: given the pace of technology, many technical skills will be obsolete within a few years, but leaders are happy to fund their development. Communication skills, however, will stay with employees throughout the rest of their careers, and despite a clear need to invest in this area, the development of these skills is often not funded at all.

Most of us in the "innovation trade" know that when it comes to products, the biggest question that we often overlook is not "Can it be built?" but "Should it be built?" The only way to answer that question, though, and potentially save our organizations from market failure, embarrassment, and the loss of hundreds of thousands, if not millions, of dollars, requires us to speak with, and listen to, the entire ecosystem. We need to consider communication just like any other skill—it must be developed and practiced to be used correctly and effectively and then embedded in everything we do, especially when it comes time to put innovation into action.

### Communication Leads to Transformation

You need to make sure people recognize innovation and understand its worth and potential throughout your organization and into the greater ecosystem. With the right messaging, you can demonstrate the value of your programs, products, and services, and how your innovation efforts play a critical role in their success. Internally, you need to have a simple message that clarifies innovation strategy and goals—both the long-term ones and the short, measurable milestones—and, when applicable, provides examples of when these have been a success. This information should be easy to comprehend and shared with all the involved players: from employees to leadership, among leadership, back to the employees and customers, and then out into the market. This "innovation messaging" must also be reiterated on a regular basis.

Every employee needs to know how your organization innovates, and why, not to mention what role they play and what is expected of them. To get these points across, try taking a new approach, not the same old boring one-way corporate messaging. Just look at the global insurance firm Assurant. With employees in fifteen countries, the firm needed a simple way to explain their strategy to employees, so they decided to gamify it with a board game. Everyone from the CEO to the mailroom clerk ended up playing it. As a result, more than 82 percent of Assurant's employees felt more engaged.[15] It was a great approach to making everyone feel included and valued, and, most importantly, they associated the strategy with something fun and exciting.

Just as in developing strategy and measuring innovation's effects, communication is essential to maintaining transparency. And transparency builds trust. Though you must highlight successes and where the company's innovation efforts are having the greatest impacts, it's equally as important to show where these efforts are falling short, why, and when. Your employees are going to know when you're not being totally forthright—they have eyes, they have ears, they'll realize when something isn't working. If you're upfront with them, you will earn their trust and, in so doing, you'll have an easier time opening them up to the possibilities of adopting innovation mindsets. If you show them that you're paying attention to innovation and are serious about its prospects, they'll be more likely to provide their input and take steps to get involved. In that way, a sense of ownership is created throughout the company.

As it's surely clear by now, innovation is high-risk, high-reward—small mistakes in messaging communication can have disastrous effects. Once you've lost the attention or respect of your audience, you have to work to get them back. The process may need to begin all over again. That's why consistency is so crucial. If regular channels of communication are open, there's a better chance of keeping everyone on the same page and connected to the end goal. Without consistent and ongoing communication, you can't transform your culture into one of innovation. The right level of communication is what will result in that ultimate change, first internally and then externally.

## Start Internally

Any innovation involves the practical art of bringing others on board. As discussed, you must convince employees and executive leadership that the time and resources redirected toward innovation are going to be well spent, not wasted. Even if you can prove that an innovation will be successful or is already showing positive results, you still need to make sure everyone hears and internalizes this good news. Innovation works, but unless you show the value, and market it to your stakeholders, no one is going to pay attention. If no one hears about the benefits, they'll assume there are none. Weak communication leads to lost messages, and your strategy will fail to receive the attention it deserves. If no data is given, people tend to just make it up, and normally what they make up is negative.

Just as innovation execution needs to be consistent so does your communication. You can't just shout out a few nice words and move on. If you try feeding people empty platitudes they're going to catch on, writing you off along with whatever you're pitching. If that "whatever" happens to be innovation, you're taking some major steps backward, and recovery will be costly. So the first step in your internal communication strategy must come from genuinely connecting with employees.

### Connect with Employees

The top three reasons people dislike their jobs are all related to problems surrounding communication: "lack of direction from management," "poor communication overall," and "constant change that is not well communicated."[16] Of course, I understand not everyone "likes" their job—there are days they hate it, sometimes love it, think it's "meh," can't believe they didn't take that other job when they had the chance, and so on. In fact, most of us probably have some type of love/hate relationship with what we do for a living. And that's fine: it's okay to have mixed feelings about our work, but it's not okay to give out mixed messages. A lack of open communication and transparency causes issues for employees, making it harder for them to get their jobs done. When they don't have clear direction, they'll be at a loss for what to do.

This lack of clarity only leads to mounting problems. People get confused, which leads to frustration. Frustration leads to anger, resentment, and disengagement. Next thing you know your teams are unhappy at work *all the time* and that love/hate relationship becomes hate/hate, and if you're the leader, that feeling might get projected onto you. At that point, good luck getting any cooperation when you bring up the "I" word. If employees don't know what they're being measured on (discussed in Chapter 3), they don't know what to focus on. If it's not fully clear that innovation is a priority, then it's never going to make it to the top of the to-do list.

If innovation is not getting across to your employees and your goals are being ignored, you need to refocus your efforts in an attempt to begin developing an environment of innovation communication. Keep in mind that this doesn't just mean a presentation on the topic; this means creating an atmosphere in which employees are actively encouraged to engage by expressing their own ideas and developing them for the benefit of the organization. Just as you need to look to employees for suggestions on strategy (as outlined in Chapter 2), you also need to support their work. If they have ideas, you want to hear them out and be able to implement them when possible. In that way, a two-way conversation develops in which everyone is thinking about, and talking about, innovation transformation.

Not every company is small enough to just hash out these ideas in a conference room or even a town hall meeting. Especially with large global organizations, there needs to be a way to connect everyone around strategy and goals. That's where employee forums, interest groups, and specific innovation forums come in handy. These outlets provide an opportunity to keep the conversation around innovation alive, kicking, and ready for more, no matter the size of the company. For example, at the media and information company Thomson Reuters, the employee communications team launched an internal video channel on their internal Innovation Network site, asking employees to submit their own videos with innovation-related content. The site became the number one most viewed site in the company's entire network, as employees at all levels exchanged their thoughts and ideas on innovation.[17]

Posting messages from the CEO, sharing customer feedback, or highlighting articles from outside media on your company's successes (and failures) can all contribute to making innovation part of an organization's culture. And none of them require a large investment either. You can just as easily utilize inexpensive online platforms to create members-only groups and forums as you can with expensive ones. Don't let tech get in the way—it's more important to find a simple solution to connect with employees, on their own terms if possible, than worry about special platforms or programs.

Forums like this provide an opportunity to develop the feedback loop previously discussed, in which employees can give their opinion, present their ideas, and share how they implemented them. The whole point is to engage as many people as possible and help them transition into an innovation mindset. If you're starting a new initiative based around innovation principles, you're going to need to get to the point where you feel like you are almost overcommunicating. Vague recommendations or suggestions are not nearly as effective as hard, straightforward direction. You don't need to become a helicopter boss, but you do need to help people stay on track. It's hard enough for most leaders who aren't used to tapping into their inner-innovation-self, but unless you can work with employees and co-workers to develop understanding and confidence, nothing is going to get done.

This confidence comes from your support and recognition, and it results in a sense of personal responsibility and a feeling of collective ownership. If you work together to set reasonable expectations and goals and communicate them through all possible channels, they're much more likely to be met, and even surpassed. Helping them to develop the right soft skills to succeed takes it even a step further. At that point, employees are becoming truly involved, which is what you're ultimately aiming for. As a leader, you want them to know that they're part of the team, the overall community within the organization—they should have some skin in the game. In doing so, they're becoming emotionally invested, engaged, and empowered, leading to pride in their work and value. As a result, they are more likely to become active advocates for your organization and brand. And let's admit it—when we see that people are happy where they work, we are more likely to respect those brands and buy from them.

Unfortunately, most employees aren't shown how their work makes an impact, especially on the company's bottom line. One survey discovered that less than half (47 percent) of workers are able to see the connection between their job's duties and the company's resulting financials.[18] If they don't realize the effect they're creating, then they may end up thinking all their work is in vain. When that's the case, that common frustration and anger arise and people start looking for the exit door.

Communication can solve this problem, reeling employees back in or, better yet, stopping a mass exodus before it starts. If you can draw a direct line from employees' efforts to innovation strategy successes, and then on to an increase in the hardest metric of them all—I'm talking money here, of course—then they will feel even more valued. A cycle begins to develop: engaged employees lead to a focus on innovation, which results in financial success, further inspiring employees to lean in to innovation further. If this cycle persists, executives are certainly going to take notice, but they'll still need some guidance from middle managers and communication teams as well.

### Show Executives the Way

As first looked at in Chapter 2, for innovation to succeed, you need to get vertical buy-in from top to bottom. Though much of your focus will be on helping to drive strategy with employees, you have to ensure that support rains down, not just trickles, from above. The key is to make innovation relevant to the business for all leaders. It doesn't matter if they're in engineering, sales, or customer experience—everyone needs to understand the importance of innovation to the organization's actual success. Communicating with leaders is essential, as they are the ones customers and employees look to as the face of your organization. In many cases, they'll have to communicate your innovation efforts to a wider audience. If you make your executives care about innovation and get their support in holding others accountable for its results, then you better believe talk of innovation is going to be greater, and much more actionable, throughout your organization.

It's hard to keep free-flowing communication open in any area. Fear of ruffling feathers or being the messenger who is shot for bringing bad news is real. We need to get over and move beyond that mindset. Difficult conversations are always more productive than easy ones because they shed light on what really needs to be done to grow. With innovation, there are additional obstacles, as executives may remain skeptical until they can be shown proven results.

So, it's time to show them.

There's probably no better way to begin than to appeal to them with the cost of inaction. Tell them about what's going on out there in the world and how detrimental inaction could be. If your company isn't investing in employees, developing partnerships, becoming part of the innovation ecosystem, you won't be able to keep up with competitors and the future won't look too bright. Just remind them of some of the companies that failed to innovate over the past decade and are now mere talking points of corporate extinction. That said, your communication doesn't need to focus on gloom and doom alone—show the positive effect that innovation is already having within your organization. And if there's nothing to show yet, provide insight into those companies that are making innovation central to their operations.

Just as with employees, try your best to avoid the same old boring approaches to communicating with executives. Maybe take a page from Lowe's, the home improvement retailer. Just like many other companies and organizations out there today getting proactively involved in developing a culture of innovation, Lowe's created its own innovation lab. When Lowe's Innovation Labs decided that they needed to double down on communicating the value of innovation to the company's leadership, they hired a team of science fiction writers, turning their ideas into a comic book. Executives loved it.[19]

Don't "go dark"—you must proactively message your status and the value that you are bringing. A regular formal progress report, quarterly or annually, is essential for the visibility of your program. For example, the Innovation Acceleration Program at Boston Children's Hospital, a nonprofit teaching hospital affiliated with Harvard University, publishes an annual report highlighting innovation projects and their impact.[20] The report is done in simple and inspiring language and is accessible to anyone who cares to take a look. If you follow suit, make sure to get these types of reports, featuring actual information, in front of your leaders.

When your teams start hitting those small, measurable milestones, you want that open corridor of communication with the executive leadership to already exist, so you can easily prove that innovation is working. If you can exhibit that goals are being achieved and metrics are being reached, your chances of continued funding are going to improve. When everything doesn't go as planned, don't panic. Just as you're meant to be honest and open with your employees, you need to be the same with executives. Explain where and why you fell short, and what the next steps are to solve the problem. When possible, highlight what's been learned in the process and where potential pivots could take place.

As communication teams reach out to the employees, they must also do so with the executives and board members too. Everyone should of course be given access to the forums or other inner-office intranet connections so everyone can share their thoughts, successes, and failures around innovation. Companywide meetings and events must keep innovation front and center as well. When executives see methodical execution and real measurable successes, they'll want more, so they will focus on them and draw attention to them throughout the company. That's really when the innovation culture begins to develop—when everyone is on the same page and acting together toward reaching common goals. This message needs to be reiterated and dialogues need to carry on to the point that the support and praise of innovation boils over and out into the rest of the world.

## Create Dialogue Externally

Just as no one will care about innovation within your company if they don't know about it, no one outside the company will care about all the progress and steps forward you've made if they don't hear about them. Communication to the rescue. It's key to work with your PR and marketing groups to take the messages that have been spread throughout your company and get them out to your customers, your current or potential partners, and the public. These messages need to maintain consistency as well, aligning the external with the internal. Also, the two-way conversation doesn't end in the office; open communication—with an emphasis on listening—needs to remain in full effect in the greater ecosystem as well.

### Talk to Your Customers

As discussed, for innovation to succeed, you need to keep lines of communication open with your employees and connect with them through as many avenues as possible. Your customers and partners—or potential customers and partners—are no different. If they know you're listening and you genuinely care about their feedback, desires, and needs, they will support you that much more. They'll start to feel like they co-own ideas behind the products and services you're developing. There are countless opportunities online and offline to develop an "omni-channel" approach to reaching them.

If your PR team stops at a press release about your company's new "innovation-focused" efforts your customers are likely to entirely miss the "news" and not recognize the actual value it brings them. Meet them where they already are: social media, company-specific message boards, email newsletters, or product review boards. As mentioned earlier, crowdsourcing is an especially effective way of working with customers as well. If applicable, you can of course share metrics, highlighting how your small steps are leading to major results. Transparency is just as dire here as it is within your company, setting customers' expectations and maintaining morale in the company's profits, revenue, growth, or sustainability.

Consumers, or citizens in the case of cities, states, and countries, can also be a great resource in deciding where to innovate next. Listen to them in the same way you listen to your employees and take their suggestions seriously. You may need to weed out some less than stellar ideas, but your customers generally know what they want and they're certainly willing to tell you—just think, there are over 113 million product reviews available on Amazon. With so much data today, you have plenty of opportunities to discover what people really want from certain products and services. You already have many connection points with your existing and prospective customers. Use these opportunities to open up a real dialogue with your customers and show them that their input matters. In the end, you each supply the other with what you're both looking for. But this two-way street doesn't end there.

### Maintain Open Dialogues with Partners

Customer-centricity is all the rage, and rightfully so, but when it comes to innovation you're looking at the entire ecosystem, not just pockets of the population. You therefore need to make sure you're also clearly communicating with your partners, especially in collaborations around innovation, as outlined in the previous chapter. Miscommunication or dropped messages could lead to failed initiatives, resentment, or confusion that could bring any accelerator or incubator to a halt, so remaining open and willing to discuss issues and ideas is imperative.

Keep in mind that co-innovation will take different forms with different partners—startups likely have different goals than universities or city governments, and all of them will have various areas of expertise that you'll want to speak to. For example, when you are working with a small company just getting off the ground, conversations around investment opportunities and scaling a product or service will be more useful to them than discussing new ways to validate research, which colleges would latch onto. Governments are going to have a greater focus on fixing specific problems for their constituents. No matter who they are and the goals they are trying to achieve, you still need to treat them as equal partners. Just because you think there's more financial gain in working with a cutting-edge startup, doesn't mean you should ignore a legacy institution. Be candid with all of them, share your experiences, and show how innovation efforts are transforming your company.

Just as your communications team members consistently stay on message with your employees and customers, you need to do the same with your partners. Show them the value that you're bringing to the table by providing real-life examples of what your company is accomplishing. Since you're going to be working with many groups (some that may come from a variety of different backgrounds), a consistent, clear message also builds your reputation and will help you overcome cultural and language barriers. Work with your communications team to create a document that your entire company can use to explain what you're all about, where you're headed, and where you're looking to collaborate in the greater innovation ecosystem. Not only does this create clarity, but it can also be used as a tool to attract potential and new partners.

You'll learn a lot from employees and customers, but you're likely to learn even more from these partners, lessons that you can return with to implement in your own organization. Just as much as we partner with others to help them, we also do so to create greater knowledge of our own that we can share internally and use to further our innovation transformation. Listening is therefore paramount—without it, no true communication can occur, which means innovation comes to a halt.

## Case Study: Instant Pot

Everyone's in a rush these days. With the speed of the Fourth Industrial Revolution, we've all tried to keep up, finding innovative new ways to save time and maximize what's most important to us, whether work, hobbies, or family. In a way, that's not much different than what people have always done. Take cooking. The microwave—invented in the 1940s—basically automated home cooking and vastly changed how people made and ate food.[21] Much earlier, literally hundreds of years, French physicist Denis Papin took the first stab at a pressure cooker, or what he called the "Steam Digester," in 1679 to speed up the cooking process.[22] But it took a former engineer from Nortel, a major Canadian telecom networking company that filed for bankruptcy in 2009, to bring a revamped version of the product into the twenty-first century.

Called the "Internet's most viral pressure cooker," the Instant Pot was developed by Robert Wang in 2008.[23] Both he and his wife were working full time and, like most of us caught up in the rat race, found that come the end of the day, cooking a full meal, especially a healthy one for their two kids, could prove to be a major challenge. With his engineering experience in hand, he started working on a new product, a much-improved version of Papin's seventeenth-century venture. He brought on some fellow telecom engineers and invested $300,000 in development, and within 18 months the first-generation version of the product was born.[24] Part pressure cooker, part crockpot, part rice cooker, part just about anything you could think of for your culinary prep needs, the Instant Pot uses a microprocessor and thermal and pressure sensor technology so you can cook meals of all kinds with little effort and time.

Wang didn't just come up with the R2D2-looking time saver by hanging around his kitchen and experimenting with his engineering buddies. Like any good innovator, he realized the importance of listening to his prospective customers' concerns and feedback. Some fretted about space in an overcrowded kitchen, others worried about burning their family's meal to a crisp.[25] The small size and burn protection mechanism of the Instant Pot spoke to both of these potential issues. The product started with five functions, but some models now have up to

(*continued*)

## Case Study: Instant Pot (*continued*)

ten, alleviating the need for many of the pots, pans, and cooking utensils that quickly take up shelf space and throw cupboards into total disarray.

The Instant Pot itself might be considered ingenious, but Wang's approach to selling it and communicating its value, getting out the word of his innovative new product, created the greatest impact in the public's adoption. He first tried a more traditional route, pitching samples of the device to retailers and at home goods conventions—the response was tepid at best. So he turned to Amazon, quickly realizing that the customer reviews would be vital to selling the Instant Pot and growing a community by word of mouth. In 2017, he claimed to have read 40,000 reviews (talk about engagement!) and he continues to review them religiously.[26]

Wang then began sending Instant Pots to influencers and bloggers, which quickly paid off as well. He also set up a Facebook page to better engage with actual end users of the product. Understanding that meals are social, and people love sharing pictures of their food, he realized social media was the best place to build that word-of-mouth marketing strategy. Through both Amazon and Facebook, he has received suggestions and positive and negative feedback that he has taken into account on subsequent iterations to improve the Instant Pot, and in the process, he's gained a larger customer base.

Wang's bold mission is to now put an Instant Pot in every kitchen, and he may just reach this goal one day. If you google Instant Pot, almost 27 million results pop up—not bad for a product that didn't hit the shelves until 2010. Instant Pot also became bigger than the product itself, maybe even bigger than the brand. It's a style of cooking that has garnered a cult-like, rabid following, with numerous cookbooks and social media sites sharing recipes and cooking advice. By listening to his audience, incorporating their ideas, and getting his product out into the world, Wang communicated his innovation's values, garnered evangelists and brand ambassadors, and actually helped solve a common problem that consumers faced. Without clear communication, he wouldn't have been able to get the product off the ground in the first place, and without consistent communication, he'd never be able to keep innovating as he has.

## Summary: Discover, Listen, Act

If communication doesn't take place, then nothing gets accomplished. Without actually researching the market and communicating with your potential customers, employees, and other stakeholders, you'll never know what problems you can solve for them to begin with. In essence, innovation rarely happens without active listening. And listening leads to clear, honest communication, the kind that is necessary both within your company and externally—you want the world to know how and why your company is innovative and what you're doing to push innovation forward. It's really all about value: If no one knows what you're doing, then they won't care, and if they don't care, then they certainly won't see any value in your work or accomplishments. Whether getting executive buy in, attracting talent and new customers, growing relationships with partners, or connecting with your employees, the strategy is essentially the same: develop constructive two-way communication not only to show innovation but to enable it as well.

Employee communications, PR, and marketing play a unique role here, one that no one else can take on with the same impact. They're specially set up to facilitate communication, so as long as they see innovation and its effects as important to your organization, they'll be willing to support it throughout the greater ecosystem as well. Even more importantly, their internal focus is absolutely necessary to developing a true culture of innovation. And that's really what all of these innovation principles are leading us to—a new way to organize a team, a company, or an environment around innovation, helping us to create the best companies and organizations possible and become the best people we can be.

### Principle

Innovation begins with listening. Your innovation vision, strategy, plan, and metrics must then be communicated appropriately both internally and externally, demonstrating the value you are creating and how your organization is capturing that value to help employees, customers, partners, and the public.

### Action

- Develop and support a communications plan that will share the vision, strategy, and value of innovation with employees, managers, executives, partners, and customers.
- Make sure communications is equal parts messaging out and listening back, actively connecting with your customers, employees, and other stakeholders

### Obstacles

Open avenues of communication and transparency are lacking in most companies, causing employees to lose focus and disengage, executives to discard innovation as a trend, and the public to lose interest in your efforts. Clear, consistent communication is rare, and normally focuses on messaging, not listening.

### Outcome

An environment in which the value of innovation is clearly communicated throughout the organization and to all external stakeholders, current and potential, and whose feedback is taken seriously in return.

## Notes

1. Ida Eikvag Groth and Vibeke Hayden, "How Norway Disrupted Sushi," *Implement Consulting Group,* November 2015, https://implementconsultinggroup.com/how-norway-disrupted-sushi/.
2. Ibid.
3. Jacob Goldstein, "Episode 651: The Salmon Taboo," *NPR: Planet Money*, June 5, 2019, https://www.npr.org/templates/transcript/transcript.php?storyId=729396914.
4. Groth and Hayden, "How Norway Disrupted Sushi."

5. Goldstein, "Episode 651."
6. Ibid.
7. Ibid.
8. Oeystein Sollesnes, "The Norwegian Campaign behind Japan's Love of Salmon Sushi," *Japan Times*, March 10, 2018, https://www.japantimes.co.jp/life/2018/03/10/food/norwegian-campaign-behind-japans-love-salmon-sushi/#.XSkVDJNKjL8.
9. Ibid.
10. https://www.statista.com/statistics/456500/daily-number-of-e-mails-worldwide/.
11. Natalie Thaïs Uomini and Georg Friedrich Meyer, "Shared Brain Lateralization Patterns in Language and Acheulean Stone Tool Production: A Functional Transcranial Doppler Ultrasound Study," *PLOS ONE*, August 30, 2013.
12. David Witt, "Only 14% of Employees Understand Their Company's Strategy and Direction," *Blanchard LeaderChat*, May 21, 2012, https://leaderchat.org/2012/05/21/only-14-of-employees-understand-their-companys-strategy-and-direction/.
13. Natalie Eisele, "Make Sure Every Worker Knows Your Company's Mission," *Business 2 Community*, April 2, 2018, https://www.business2community.com/human-resources/make-sure-every-worker-knows-companys-mission-02040790.
14. Emma Charlton, "These are the 10 Most In-demand Skills of 2019, According to LinkedIn," *World Economic Forum*, January 14, 2019, https://www.weforum.org/agenda/2019/01/the-hard-and-soft-skills-to-futureproof-your-career-according-to-linkedin/.
15. Melissa Kivett, "Why Insurance Firm Assurant Designed a Strategy Game for Employees to Play," *Innovation Leader*, February 24, 2016, https://www.innovationleader.com/why-insurance-firm-assurant-designed-a-strategy-game-for-employees-to-play/.

16. Tim Eisenhauer, "Why Lack of Communication Has Become the Number One Reason People Quit," *The Next Web*, November 8, 2015, https://thenextweb.com/insider/2015/11/08/why-lack-of-communication-has-become-the-number-one-reason-people-quit/.

17. Cary Burch, "How a Video Series Is Spreading Innovation at Thomson Reuters," *Innovation Leader*, November 13, 2014, https://www.innovationleader.com/how-an-internal-video-series-is-spreading-innovation-at-thomson-reuters/.

18. Lisa Quast, "Four Ways to Help Your Employees Understand How They Contribute To The Company's Bottom Line," *Forbes*, December 19, 2016, https://www.forbes.com/sites/lisaquast/2016/12/19/four-ways-to-help-your-employees-understand-how-they-contribute-to-the-companys-bottom-line.

19. Corinne Ruff, "Why Lowe's Uses Comic Books to Guide Innovation," *Retail Dive*, October 5, 2017, https://www.retaildive.com/news/why-lowes-uses-comic-books-to-guide-innovation/506504/.

20. Naomi Fried, "Naomi Fried: My 3 Highest-impact Programs," *Innovation Leader*, September 14, 2013, https://www.innovationleader.com/naomi-fried-my-3-highest-impact-programs/.

21. Matt Blitz, "The Amazing True Story of How the Microwave Was Invented by Accident," *Popular Mechanics*, February 24, 2016, https://www.popularmechanics.com/technology/gadgets/a19567/how-the-microwave-was-invented-by-accident/.

22. Discover Pressure Cooking, "The History of Pressure Cooking," discoverpressurecooking.com, 2019, http://www.discoverpressurecooking.com/history.html.

23. Arturo Chang, "Former Nortel Engineer Behind Viral 'Instant Pot,'" *BNN Bloomberg,* March 17, 2017, https://www.bnnbloomberg.ca/former-nortel-engineer-behind-viral-instant-pot-1.698935.

24. Margaret Rhodes, "Fired from His Own Startup, This Founder Invented Amazon's Hit Product of 2016," *Inc.*, June 2017, https://www.inc.com/magazine/201706/margaret-rhodes/double-insight-instant-cooking-pot-design-awards-2017.html.

25. Tom Huddleston Jr., "How Instant Pot Became a Kitchen Appliance with a Cult Following and a Best-seller on Amazon," *CNBC: Make It*, November 26, 2018, https://www.cnbc.com/2018/11/26/how-instant-pot-became-a-kitchen-appliance-with-a-cult-following.html.

26. Ibid.

# Conclusion: Business as Usual

Despite all the praise showered on innovation throughout these pages, make no mistake: I stand by what I wrote in the introduction: "innovation" is still an overused horrible buzzword (which, by the way, I use more than 850 times in this book). Over the years, how we perceive the term has changed, gotten lost, or been repackaged and rebranded in a way that causes confusion and anxiety or inspires eyerolls and chuckles. With all the skepticism and misconceptions, and the incorrect notions of what it means to "be innovative," we'd probably all be a little happier if we could come up with another term and move on to the business at hand. In the future, maybe we can call it the "word that shall not be named" or, better yet, "business as usual," since that's really what we're striving for here—making real innovation part of our everyday lives.

It also doesn't *actually* matter what we call it. What matters is that once it's woven into the fabric of an organization's culture, it becomes so intuitive, so ever present and unidentifiable, that it needs no name at all. Remember, innovation is an attitude, a mindset, even an art, not a PR strategy or campaign slogan. It's time that we treat it with the respect and reverence it deserves—because without it, we're all screwed.

Similarly, we can refer to "change" as whatever we want. Call it "disruption"; call it "a new industrial revolution"; call it "progress," "transformation," or "the movement of hands along a clock." However you refer to it, just know that it's constant, and its demands cannot be met if we don't stay prepared—one, two, three, or even ten steps ahead. We must grow and advance as companies and organizations, but also as individuals, as a society, and as a global community together. The opportunities and threats of tomorrow are requiring us to pay attention and step up today. If we're scared of the future, unprepared or apathetic, living in denial or fear of change, fear of innovation, then we're all doomed. What we really need to do is dispense with fear, become aware and proactive, and empower ourselves and others to figure out the solutions to the problems we're facing today and beyond. What we need is a truly bold culture—a culture of fearless innovation.

No one can do it alone, and luckily, no one has to. Most of us are social beings, and outcomes are always better when we work together. Innovators are behind all breakthroughs throughout history—from science to art and everything in between—but only because they were willing to co-innovate with others. Together, we grow and evolve, and we need our understanding of "innovation" to grow and evolve as well.

We must start by recognizing innovation as a constant. With exponential changes in technology, speed has become the name of the game and we need to keep up, remain relevant, and succeed far into the future. We can't do that without innovation, which in turn requires strong leadership, strategy, and participation from all. It is absolutely imperative that no one ever has a monopoly on innovation within any organization. Innovation is like a dance, in which partners work together to create a movement bigger than themselves, a fluid set of motions that come across as, daresay, beautiful. Of course, one of the partners must lead, directing the steps, twists, and turns, but without one another, the dance falls apart. No matter our job titles, where we are in our careers, or the size of our organizations, everyone needs to take part in innovation in one way or another, and that can only come through a sense of empowerment, engagement, and execution. We need to plan together, strategize together, and dream big together. After all, form follows thought, and if we can imagine it, we can create it.

We must show others that innovation works, otherwise they will lose faith and shift their energy and attention elsewhere. To do that, we need be aligned on strategy and goals with our stakeholders. These goals do not amount to some "great disruption," and, in fact, having "disruption" as the primary goal will likely only lead to failure. Simplicity is key, but so is a wide range of voices, opinions, and ideas. Innovation therefore demands diversity and inclusion, creating opportunities to connect with others, listen to one another, and learn from one another's experiences.

Innovation wants to be free: when we partner with others, we create a greater ecosys that benefits us all. There's really no "innovation" that isn't "co-innovation"—it can't take place in a bubble, and it can't be cordoned off to one or two individuals. It requires constant communication, both talking and listening. If no one knows what we're doing, no one is going to care. Without communication, innovation just won't take place.

But it must, because even though it sounds grandiose and melodramatic, innovation is what will save this world, just as it has in the past and will in the future. It's real, it's effective, and it's how humanity will continue to overcome challenges and prosper. We want innovation without regrets, innovation that will enact change and be a positive force. We want true innovation, the kind that can't be dumbed down to a few pseudo-inspirational words on a dry erase board or a talking point in a quarterly meeting. So it's about time we all get beyond the buzzword, leave the skepticism behind, focus on the signal instead of the noise, and *get to work.*

Now that's a mindset worth embracing.

As I am sure you've picked up by now, I am passionate about this topic, and I'd like to think that I've learned a lot about it over the years, but I of course realize that I don't know everything. I always look forward to learning more from others, and to that end I'd love to hear from you about what most resonated with you in this book and what didn't. More importantly, feel free to connect and let me know how I can help you capture new opportunities or solve the problems you're facing—innovation only takes place when we work together, and I'm here to help. Reach out to me at alex@alexgoryachev.com.

# About the Author

*Form follows thought, and if we can imagine it, we can create it*

Alex Goryachev is an award-winning leader who spearheads innovation initiatives that deliver clear, tangible, measurable, and sustainable results. With more than 20 years of global experience at pioneering startups and major public companies, Alex has remained true to his lifelong passion of seamlessly transforming seemingly unrelated ideas into pragmatic end-to-end solutions.

Throughout his career, Alex has been known as a practical visionary and risk taker who gets things done in a win-together way. Alex is a managing director of Cisco's Co-Innovation Centers. He is not a stranger to making change in large companies – at Cisco he has created the global network of Co-Innovation Centers from scratch, along with an award-winning company wide portfolio of innovation programs for employees. Previously, Alex focused on developing emerging business models in the entertainment industry at Napster, the revolutionary music sharing service, as well as at Liquid Audio, which pioneered digital rights management.

Alex and his initiatives have received numerous industry awards. Also a regular contributor to *Forbes, Chief Executive Magazine*, and other business and tech industry media, Alex is sought after as an expert on innovation and culture transformation. He frequently speaks at industry forums such as the Commonwealth Club, Conference Board, and TEDx, among many others. Alex loves turning complexity into simplicity by sharing knowledge, mentoring, and demystifying innovation.

Learn more and connect with Alex at alexgoryachev.com.

# Index


## A

Academia:
  co-innovation with, 123–124
  communication with, 168
  Internet developed in, 111
Accelerators, innovation, 117–119
Accenture, 74
Accidental innovation, 60
Activity metrics, 51–53
Aetna, 46, 52
Affordability, of technology, 9–10
Airbus, 15
Airports, 76
*Alice in Wonderland* (Carroll), 32
Allan, Crawford, 125
Amazon, 72, 74, 112, 170
Ambiguity, 37
American Airlines, 58–59
Amsterdam, 70
Android system, 112
Animikii, 13
Anthem, 123
AOL, 4
Apple, 26
Association of Licensed Automobile Manufacturers, 90
Association of Southeast Asian Nations (ASEAN), 25–26
Assurant, 159
Atlanta, Georgia, 148
AT&T, 123
Audible, 72
Audiobooks, 72–73
Automobiles, introduction of, 14–15

## B

Back-office work, 138–139
Ballmer, Steve, 111, 112
Barclays, 118
B-corps (Benefit Corporations), 13, 120, 121
Bell, Alexander Graham, 89–90
Bell Patent Association, 89–90
Bell Telephone Company, 89–90
Benefit Corporations (B-corps), 13, 120, 121
Ben & Jerry's, 120
Berkshire Hathaway Energy, 74
Berners-Lee, Tim, 111
Bitmain Technologies, 1
BlackBerry, 4
Blizzard Entertainment, 7
Blockbuster, 4
Bloomberg, Michael R., 148
Bloomberg LP, 148
Bloomberg Philanthropies, 148–149
BMW, 26
Boeing, 15, 58–59, 123
Boston Children's Hospital, 165
Boston Consulting Group, 98
Brick-and-mortar retailers, 5
Build phase, of innovation program, 105
ByteDance, 1

## C

Carlsbad, California, 122, 140
Carroll, Lewis, 32
Case Western Reserve University, 45
Centralized innovation teams, 145
CERN (European Organization for Nuclear Research), 111
Change:
  disruption as, 71
  increasing speed of, 2
  rapid speed of, 18
  responses to, 5–8
  terminology for, 177–178
  working with, 8–10

Change agents, 141
Chen, Steve, 8
Chick-fil-A, 123
Chief innovation officers, 135–150
  Bloomberg Philanthropies case study, 148–149
  hiring of, 139–142
  innovation governance processes managed by, 142–144
  innovation orchestrated by, 137–139
  innovation teams managed by, 144–147
  roles of, 135–137
Chief People Officer, 100
Circque de Soleil, 49, 50, 52
Circuses, 49
Cisco, 26, 102–105
Cisco International Internship Program, 124
Cities:
  chief innovation officers hired by, 139–140
  co-innovation with, 121–122
  i-teams in, 148–149
CNET, 80
Coca-Cola, 117–118
Co-Create IKEA, 128
Cohen, Ben, 120
Co-innovation, 111–129
  with academia, 123–124
  with cities and governments, 121–122, 148–149
  communication in, 167–168, 179
  and cross-functional work, 97
  with customers, 120–121, 167
  IKEA case study, 127–128
  importance of, 178
  innovation accelerators and incubators, 117–119
  with nonprofits, 124–126
  and open-source movement, 111–114
  with other companies, 114–117
Collaboration, 73
Communication, 153–172
  about urgency of innovation, 15
  in co-innovation, 179
  in corporate-startup partnerships, 116
  digital, 156–157
  external, 166–168
  importance of, 155–156
  Instant Pot case study, 169–170
  internal, 160–166
  and Norwegian salmon, 153–155
  skills and capabilities for, 156–159
Communities, improving, 122, 148–149
Commuter drones, 15
Companies:
  co-innovation with other, 114–117
  co-innovation with startups and established, 114–117
Competition:
  and co-innovation, 113, 126
  diversity as advantage in, 98–99
Confidence, developing, 162–163
Conformation bias, 35
Connexion, 58–59
Cook, Tim, 136
Corporate-startup partnerships, 114–117
Creativity, 48
Cross-functional work:
  by chief innovation officers, 136, 140–141
  innovation teams doing, 146–147
  overcoming silos with, 95–98
Crowdsourcing, 120–121
Culture:
  asking employees about, 33
  creating, with communication, 165–166
  improved with diversity, 98
  and innovation, 63
  set by HR, 102
Customers:
  co-innovation with, 120–121, 127–128, 167
  communication with, 166–167
  involving, in innovation, 17

## D

Data collection and publication:
  transparency in, 38–39
  at Wikimedia Foundation, 40–41
De Beers Group, 118
Decentralized innovation teams, 146
Delaktif, 128
Delivery services, 79–80
Delta Air Lines, 58–59, 123
Deora, Tanuj, 75
Developing world, 12
Digital communication, 156–157
Digital platforms, 9

Disengagement, 29–30
Disruption, 69–84
  duty-free shopping as, 69–71
  Dyson case study, 81–82
  and focus on value, 78–81
  ideas about, 71–74
  innovation vs., 83
  in music industry, 7
  as opportunity, 74–76
  and pragmatic innovation, 77–78
  in sports, 7–8
Diversity:
  in hybrid innovation teams, 147
  in innovation teams, 97–102
  necessary for innovation, 179
  at Wikimedia Foundation, 40–41
Dixon, Tom, 128
DNA analysis, 10
Dover, 123
Drucker, Peter, 48
Dubai, United Arab Emirates, 70
Durvy, Mathilde, 103
Duty-free shopping, 69–71, 76
Dyson, 81–82
Dyson, Sir James, 81–82

## E

eBay, 112, 125
E-books, 72
Economic Development Board (Singapore), 26
Ecosystems, engagement with, 119–120, 126
Edison, Thomas, 6, 89, 90
1871, 124–125
Electric Vehicle Company, 90
Emerson, 123
Emmons, Scott, 138
Employees:
  communicating with, 157–163
  engagement of, 29–30, 55
  finding and hiring, 100–101
  information shared by, 28
  listening to, 32–38
  responsible for innovation, 93, 102–105
  retention of, 101
  transparency in data collection with, 38–39
Employment, 100–101
*Encyclopedia Britannica,* 39
Energy industry, 74–75
Engagement, 29–30
  communication to create, 162–163
  in corporate-startup partnerships, 116
  with ecosystems, 119–120, 126
Enron, 47
Enterprise Innovation Institute, 123
Esports, 7–8
Ethnic and racial diversity, 98–99
Etsy, 125
European Organization for Nuclear Research (CERN), 111
Execution:
  asking employees about, 34
  as component of innovation, 26–27, 92–93
  of innovation, 78
Executives, 163–166. *See also* management
Exercise, 3
Exit polls, 35–36
External communication, 155, 166–168

## F

Facebook, 4, 74, 112, 125, 127, 170
"Fake innovation," 47
Farmers' Anti-Automobile Society of Pennsylvania, 15
FDI (foreign direct investment), 26
Feedback:
  from employees, 36
  on viability of ideas, 56–57
First Industrial Revolution, 1
Flexibility, 59–60
Ford, Henry, 6, 15, 90
Foreign direct investment (FDI), 26
Forums, for connecting with employees, 161–162
Forward-looking mindset:
  in business planning, 54
  of chief innovation officers, 141–142
  in governance processes, 143–144
  importance of keeping, 4–5, 177–178
Fourth Industrial Revolution, 1–3, 12
Friedman, Milton, 136–137
Funding, of initiatives, 142–143
Fund phase, of innovation program, 104–105
Furniture, open-source, 128
Future Lab (LEGO), 17

## G


G, Kenny, 6
GemFair, 118
Gender diversity, 99
General Mills, 46
Genomics, personal, 10
Georgia Institute of Technology, 123
Georgia Pacific, 123
GitHub, 112
Global Coalition to End Wildlife Trafficking Online, 125
Goals:
- aligned, with stakeholders, 178–179
- employee feedback informing, 36–37
- as first step in innovation, 31–32
- specific and actionable, 39

Google, 4, 46, 74, 125
Governance processes, 142–144
Governments:
- chief innovation officers hired by, 139–140
- co-innovation with, 121–122
- communication with, 168
- i-teams in, 148–149

Graham, David, 140
Gray, Elisha, 89
Great Place to Work, 98
Greenfield, Jerry, 120
Grove, Andy, 14
Growth, as goal of innovation, 32


## H


Harvard Business School, 113
*Harvard Business Study Review,* 143
Hawaii, 70
Headspace app, 48–49
Hierarchy of needs, 11
Highest-paid person's opinion (HiPPO), 29
Home Depot, 123
Honesty, 56–58. *See also* transparency
Honeywell, 123
HR, partnering with, 100–103
Human aspirations, as goal of innovation, 31
Hybrid innovation teams, 146–147


## I


IBM 350, 10
Ideate phase, of innovation program, 104
Ignoring change, 5, 16
IKEA, 127–128
Impact metrics, 51–53
Inclusion:
- in innovation teams, 97–102
- necessary for innovation, 179

Incubators, innovation, 117–119
Inflight Connectivity Survey, 59
Information, sharing, 27–28, 93–97, 111–112
Information silos, 93–97
Information technology (IT), 135
Inmarsat, 59
"Innovate everywhere challenge" (Cisco), 102
Innovation, 1–19
- accidental, 60
- communicating with leadership about, 164
- as constant, 178
- disruption vs., 71, 83
- fake, 47
- importance of, 1–3
- increased with diversity, 97–98
- invention vs., 92–93
- lack of, 3–5, 27–30
- LEGO case study, 16–17
- metrics for, 50–54
- orchestrated by chief innovation officers, 137–139
- pragmatic, 77–78
- and purpose, 10–13
- and responses to change, 5–8
- terminology for, 177
- timing of, 14–16, 58–60, 80
- working with change, 8–10

Innovation Acceleration Program (Boston Children's Hospital), 165
Innovation accelerators and incubators, 117–119
Innovation governance processes, 142–144
Innovation index, 51
Innovation Leader, 51, 52, 62
Innovation teams, 89–107
- centralized, 145
- Cisco case study, 102–105
- decentralized, 146
- fostering diversity and inclusion in, 97–102
- hybrid, 146–147
- invention vs. innovation, 92–93

and lonely innovator myth, 89–91
managed by chief innovation officers, 144–147
and silos, 93–97
structure of, 144–145
"Innovation theater," 48
Instacart, 79, 80
Instant Pot, 169–170
Intel, 14
Interdepartmental work, 97. *See also* cross-functional teams
Internal communication, 155, 160–166
International Fund for Animal Welfare, 125
International travel, 61–62
Invention, 92–93
iPhone, 10, 59
*Iron Chef,* 154
Ishinabe, Yutaka, 154
IT (information technology), 135
I-teams, 148–149

## J

Japan, 153–155
Jazz, 6

## K

Kamprad, Ingvar, 127
Katsoudas, Fran, 104
Kaufer, Caroline, 61
Kaufer, Stephen, 61–62
Kennedy, John F., 29–30
Keyes, Jim, 4
Keysight Technologies, 123
Kickstarter, 13
Kirsner, Scott, 51, 52, 137–138
Knowledge-based economy, 100–101
Kodak, 4
Korn Ferry, 101

## L

Laliberté, Guy, 49
Leaders:
communicating with employees, 160–163
communication with, 163–166
information shared by, 28
innovation championed by, 15–16
of innovation teams, 91
Leadership, 25–42
and lack of innovation, 27–30
listening to employees, 32–38
in Singapore, 25–27
taking responsibility, 30–32
transparency in data collection and publication, 38–39
trust in, 35
Wikimedia Foundation case study, 39–41
LEGO, 16–17
Lianjia, 1
Light bulbs, 89
Linux, 111–113
Listening, to employees, 32–38
London School of Economics, 59
London Stock Exchange, 112
Lonely innovator myth, 89–91
Lööf, Torbjörn, 128
Lowe's, 164–165
Lowe's Innovation Labs, 165
Lufthansa, 58–59
Lyft, 75

## M

McKinsey, 98–99
Majgaard, Christian, 17
Malls, 5
Management:
communicating with employees, 160–163
cross-functional work methods of, 96
involving, in innovation management, 103–104
metrics viewed by, 53, 55–56
Marketing teams, 166–167
Maryland, 139
Maslow, Abraham, 10–11
Maslow's hierarchy of needs, 11
Mayo Clinic, 46
Meditation, 45–46, 48–49
Memphis, Tennessee, 148
Menlo Park, New Jersey, 90
Mental silos, 95
Metrics, 45–64
as drivers of change, 27–28
importance of using, 47–50
for innovation, 50–54
for mindfulness practices, 45–47
and timing of innovation, 58–60
transparency in use of, 54–58
TripAdvisor case study, 61–62

Microsoft, 26, 112, 125
Microwaves, 169
Middle management:
  cross-functional work methods of, 96
  information shared by, 28
Mindfulness practices, 45–49
Mission, employee understanding of, 29, 157
Morale, 38–39
Morse, Samuel F. B., 89, 90
Motorola, 4
Mozilla Firefox, 112
Murgian, Madhumita, 41
Music, innovation in, 6
Music industry, disruption in, 7, 73
Musk, Elon, 91
Myspace, 4

## N

Napster, 7, 73
NASA:
  employee engagement at, 29–30
  Linux used by, 112
  "night light" maps released by, 11–12
NASDAQ, 112
Nath, Jay, 139
Natura Cosméticos SA, 13
NCR, 123
Needs, hierarchy of, 11
Neiman Marcus, 138
Nespresso, 58, 59
Nestle, 58
Netflix, 74
New Orleans, Louisiana, 148
New York City, New York, 148
New York Stock Exchange, 112
New York Times, 6
NFL, 7–8
"Night light" maps, 11–12
Nokia, 4
Nonprofits, 124–126
Nortel, 169
Norwegian salmon, 153–155

## O

Obesity, 3
Office politics, 147
Online sports, 7–8
Open-source movement, 111–114
Operational efficiency, as goal of innovation, 31–32
Opportunity, disruption as, 74–76
O'Regan, Brendan, 70, 71, 76
Our People Deal (Cisco), 102
Overwatch League, 7, 8

## P

Papin, Denis, 169
Partnerships:
  communication in, 167–168
  corporate-startup, 114–117
  with HR, 100–102
  innovation with, 17
Patagonia, 13
Patents, 92–93
PayPal, 112
Perel, Esther, 46
Personal genomics, 10
Pinterest, 1
Pokémon Go, 58
Polaroid, 4
Port wine, 60
Postmates, 79, 80
Pragmatic innovation, 77–78
Prioritization, 37
"Project Japan," 154
PR teams, 166–167
Public utilities, 74–75
Publishing industry, 72–73
Purpose, 10–13
Purpose-driven businesses, 12–13

## R

R&D:
  by Thomas Edison, 90
  involving customers in, 120–121
  at LEGO, 17
  in Singapore, 26
Record Industry Association of America (RIAA), 7
Regulation, 7, 75
Renewable energy sources, 74, 75
Responsibility:
  and confidence, 162
  for innovation, 136–137
  taking, 30–32

Revenue:
as impact metric, 52
from solving problems and creating value, 79
RIAA (Record Industry Association of America), 7
Ridesharing companies, 75–76
Ringling Bros. and Barnum & Bailey Circus, 49
Robbins, Chuck, 104
RocketSpace, 118
Ryan ToysReview (YouTube channel), 8, 16

## S

Sacramento, California, 139–140
Salmon, 153–155
Sanborn, David, 6
San Diego, California, 140
San Francisco, California, 139
Sanger, Larry, 40
Savings, as impact metric, 52
*SB Nation,* 7
Schank, Joshua L., 140
Schools, diversity in, 99
*Scientific American,* 99
Scribd, 72
Sears, 4
Second Industrial Revolution, 1–2
Selden, George, 90–91
Self-actualization, 11
Shaming change, 5–6
Shannon, Ireland, 70
Shannon airport, 70
Siemens, 123
*The Silo Effect* (Tett), 94–95
Silos, 93–97
breaking down, 103–104
and centralized innovation teams, 145
chief innovation officers in, 140–141
and decentralized innovation teams, 146
Singapore, 25–27
Sivak, Brian, 139
Smart Electric Power Alliance, 75
Smartphones, addiction to, 46
Social impact, of corporations, 12–13
Social media, 170
Socioeconomic diversity, 99
Solar energy, 74
Sony, 94–95
Southern Company, 123
South Korea, 70
SpaceX, 1
Sports, disruption in, 7–8
Spotify, 73, 74
Stagnation, 27–30
Stakeholders:
communication with, 155–156
goals and strategies aligned with, 178–179
Stanley Black & Decker, 123
Startups:
co-innovation with established companies and, 114–117
communication with, 168
technology easing barriers for, 10
Station Houston, 124, 125
Ste-Croix, Gilles, 49
Stewart, Louis, 139–140
Strategy:
aligned, with stakeholders, 178–179
asking employees about, 34
communication necessary for, 156
disruption as, 72
publishing clear, 39
Structure, of innovation teams, 144–145
Survival, as goal of innovation, 31
Sushi, 153–155

## T

Taking responsibility, 30–32
Talent, finding and hiring, 100–101
Team values, 34–35
Techno-FOMO, 78
Techno-junkies, 46
Technology:
addiction to, 46
affordability of, 9–10
as focus of innovation, 78–79
in music industry, 73
Techstarts, 118
Telegraphs, 89
Telephones, 89
Tencent Internet, 17
Tett, Gillian, 94–95
"Thinking disruptively," 71–74
Third Industrial Revolution, 2

Thomas Reuters, 161–162
Thurman, J. S., 82
*Thursday Night Football,* 7
Timing, of innovation, 14–16, 58–60, 80
Tokyo Stock Exchange, 112
Torvalds, Linus, 111
Tourism, 61
Toys R Us, 4
TRAFFIC, 125
Transformation, 158–159
Transparency:
  and communication, 159
  in communications with customers, 167
  in corporate-startup partnerships, 115
  in data collection and publication, 38–39
  provided by governance processes, 142
  required for innovation, 33
  in use of metrics, 54–58
  at Wikimedia Foundation, 40–41
Transportation industry, 75–76
TripAdvisor Media Group, 61–62
Trust:
  in corporate-startup partnerships, 115
  in leadership, 35
23andMe, 1

## U

Uber, 1, 75
Unicorns, 1–3
United Airlines, 58–59
Urgency, in innovation, 14, 18
US Department of Defense, 111
US Marine Corps, 46
US Patent and Trademark Office, 92

## V

Vail, Alfred, 90
Validate phase, of innovation program, 104
Value:
  creating, by employees, 101–102
  creating, with innovation, 74
  and disruption, 78–81
Visual Networking Index, 9
Vox Media, 7

## W

Wales, Jimmy, 40
Walkman, 94
Walmart, 112
Wang, Robert, 169–170
Washington, Grover, Jr., 6
Watson, Thomas, 89–90
Webex, 156
Webvan, 80
Weex, 118
Weisgall, Jonathan, 74
Wen Wan Tian Xia, 125
Western Union, 90
WeWork, 1
Wi-Fi coverage, in airplanes, 58–59
Wikipedia, 39–41, 112
Wonolo, 118
World Food Programs Innovation Accelerator, 125
World Wildlife Fund (WWF), 125

## X

Xerox, 4

## Y

Yew, Lee Kuan, 25–27
YouTube, 8, 73

## Z

Zhongyikupia, 125
Zhuanzhuan, 125
Zuckerberg, Mark, 127